This Billy Graham Evangelistic Association
special edition is published with permission
from Zondervan Publishing House.

To Sandy
from Betty Holley
Christmas 1999

Corrie ten Boom at the microphone, broadcasting for Trans World Radio.
(photo credit: Hans van der Steen, used by permission of Trans World Radio,
Netherlands and Belgium)

Corrie ten Boom

Reflections of God's Glory

NEWLY DISCOVERED MEDITATIONS BY
THE AUTHOR OF *THE HIDING PLACE*

ZondervanPublishingHouse
Grand Rapids, Michigan

A Division of HarperCollins*Publishers*

Contents

Acknowledgments

Special thanks to:

Rinse Postuma, Director, Trans World Radio voor Nederland en België (Netherlands and Belgium), for special permission to translate and publish these manuscripts in English;

Clara M. van Dijk, Trans World Radio voor Nederland en België, for organizing, researching, and editing the original Dutch manuscripts;

Claire L. Rothrock, Trans World Radio-Europe, The Netherlands, for translation of all manuscripts from Dutch to English;

Hans van der Steen, Retired Director, Trans World Radio voor Nederland en België, for his valuable assistance to this project and for sharing many insights into the life and ministry of Corrie ten Boom gained from his personal relationship with Corrie formed through years of co-producing her radio broadcasts.

Tom Watkins, Trans World Radio-North America, for initiating and overseeing this project, and for editing the final manuscript.

Introduction

Dinner was over and the clean up underway. Having guests for dinner was a very commonplace occurrence in the Lowell household on the island of Bonaire in the Caribbean. But on this night our four children quickly recognized that this was no ordinary visitor.

She insisted the kids call her "Tante" (Auntie) Corrie. After excusing herself to the living room, she sat in an old wooden rocker, opened a large purse, and pulled out a purple piece of cloth. Corrie ten Boom invited the children to sit at her feet and proceeded to talk about life—her life—and the challenges she and her family faced during World War II in her German-occupied town of Haarlem in the Netherlands.

As she spoke, she slowly unfolded the purple cloth in her hands and revealed hundreds of strings tied in knots pulled through the cloth. It all looked so random. She showed the children how the strings didn't seem to make sense from where they sat at her feet on the floor of the living room. "That's the whole point," she exclaimed. She said it was because of our limited vision, our limited perspective of what God is doing in our lives, that we question Him. At that point Tante Corrie slowly turned the purple tangled mess around to reveal a beautiful tapestry: a crown of gold with multi-colored jewels.

"This," she said, "is what God sees ... from His perspective ... a masterpiece!"

During a visit to Bonaire in 1973, Corrie ten Boom shared this now-famous illustration of God's sovereignty. She had begun broadcasting radio messages in her native Dutch language to the Netherlands over Trans World Radio in 1966. Now, broadcasts had also been added to the Dutch-speaking Antilles islands from our station on Bonaire, and she wanted to see the station first-hand.

Fast forward, for a moment, to a cool, overcast midsummer day in 1996—thirteen years after Corrie's death. One of our staff members from the United States was visiting Trans World Radio's office in Voorthuizen, the Netherlands, when another, quite dramatic, introduction took place. As this guest was handed a book of Corrie ten Boom's radio messages published in Dutch by TWR–Netherlands and saw a stack of Corrie's typewritten radio scripts in a corner of the office there, the realization hit that no English-speaking person had ever had the benefit of hearing or reading these messages penned by a true giant of the Christian faith.

Thus began the odyssey that led to the publishing of *Reflections of God's Glory*, a collection of twenty-three radio messages Corrie aired in Dutch over Trans World Radio beginning three decades ago, never before translated into English.

Yet, the story of Corrie ten Boom goes back much further than either Voorthuizen or Bonaire. It was on February 28, 1944, that the lives of the Ten Boom family of Haarlem changed forever. On that day, Corrie, her father, her older sister, and thirty-five other people were arrested and sent to a Nazi concentration camp for not disclosing the whereabouts of six Jews hidden in a secret room attached to her bedroom. Corrie, the daughter of a watchmaker, and her devoutly Christian family dedicated much of their efforts toward shielding Jews from Nazi persecution during the German occupation of the Netherlands in World War II. They were imprisoned and subjected to the atrocities of the Ravensbrück concentration camp in Germany, where Corrie's father and sister, Betsie, died. Corrie was inexplicably released after ten months of incarceration. She later found out that an order had been given at the end of the very week of her release to kill all women her age and older. God had used an error in prison paperwork as the catalyst to release her.

Corrie's unlikely voice arose from the ashes of post-World War II Europe, proclaiming the transforming message of God's love and forgiveness over the airwaves of Trans World Radio, an international Christian broadcasting ministry founded in the United States in 1952. She is most closely identified with her best-selling book *The Hiding Place*, which was later made into a full-length movie, and she gained worldwide acclaim as a Christian writer and speaker for her deep yet practical spiritual insights gleaned from her life experiences. At the time of her death in 1983, Corrie had written nine books, spoken in more than sixty countries, and produced five films.

Twenty-two years after her release from Ravensbrück, Corrie had the rare privilege of beginning a ministry of broadcasting the Good News of God's redeeming love via a powerful transmitting site in Monte Carlo utilized by Trans World Radio. Ironically, the Monte Carlo station was originally built by Adolph Hitler for his Nazi propaganda machine, but never used for his sinister purposes. Instead, God used it as an open door for Corrie to proclaim to millions worldwide her story of how God's grace sustained her during her deepest hours of despair and how He empowered her to forgive those responsible for the deaths of her father and sister.

Later, the broadcast followed from TWR–Bonaire as well as from TWR–Swaziland in Africa. Her messages were also copied onto cassettes and put into print. In addition to her popular radio talks, the text of *The Hiding Place* was broadcast over TWR–Monte Carlo and TWR–Bonaire.

Throughout the years since the initial broadcast in 1954 from Tangier, Morocco, and its first program from Monte Carlo in 1960, TWR has been blessed with missions-minded broadcasters such as Corrie ten Boom. Today, more than 250 cooperating broadcasters worldwide air their programs via TWR.

Utilizing forty transmitters from twelve primary sites and by satellite to three continents, TWR broadcasts more than 1,200 hours of gospel programs each week in over 140 languages. Each year more than 1.4 million letters are received from listeners in over 160 countries.

Radio is personal and private. It overcomes geographical, political, religious, social, and educational barriers—oftentimes in places inaccessible to missionaries or where open evangelism is risky, restricted, or banned. It also speaks the language of the intended audience. As a result, missionary radio is one the most cost-effective ways to reach people for Jesus Christ.

To discover more about the global life-changing ministry of Trans World Radio, you can write to TWR at P.O. Box 8700, Cary, NC 27512, or P.O. Box 310, London, Ontario, N6A 4W1. Or you can email us at info@twr.org. You can also learn more through the Internet at www.twr.org.

It is a singular privilege that Trans World Radio has been given, sixteen years after Corrie's death, to have a part in bringing to readers in the United States and around the world what are, in effect, fresh, new insights from the pen of Corrie ten Boom. The timeless meditations in this book are the same rich, practical applications into living the Christian life that a generation of those familiar with Corrie's ministry have come to love and expect. It is our desire that a new generation of readers will come to love and appreciate with equal fervor the unique and insightful qualities of the writings of Corrie ten Boom.

THOMAS J. LOWELL, PRESIDENT, TRANS WORLD RADIO

CARY, NORTH CAROLINA

NOVEMBER 1998

Foreword

We were in the middle of a Trans World Radio-Netherlands board meeting, being of course carried on in the Dutch language. Suddenly I heard a voice say in English, "Lord, this is really a big problem we have here." It was Corrie ten Boom who was seated next to me, and who quite naturally switched from talking to the board in Dutch to talking to the Lord in English. This was so typically Corrie. She had that refreshingly unique, practical, simple, spiritual walk with her Lord that allowed her to move in a carefree way from grappling with a problem to involving her Lord in a solution.

The story of Corrie ten Boom and Trans World Radio actually started in 1965 at a Trans World Radio triennial conference in Monte Carlo attended by our Dutch director, Hans van der Steen. Music at that conference was supplied by the Peter van Woerden family. On one of the days of the conference, Peter came to Hans and handed him some messages from his Aunt Corrie ten Boom, suggesting that perhaps he would want to use them over the air in the Trans World Radio Dutch programs.

Upon his return to Holland, Hans contacted Corrie to request permission to use the material. Corrie's response was, "Why don't you come and let's talk?" When they got together, one of the first questions Corrie asked Hans was, "How did you join TWR?"

The story of Hans and Janny van der Steen's leaving the Phillips Company, and by faith joining Trans World Radio to establish our partner organization in The Netherlands, is an unbelievable testimony of God's miraculous provision. For example, the studio equipment for the first TWR-Netherlands recording studio came from the Phillips Company as they sent Hans on his way to his new life calling.

Once, even a new car was delivered to their door by an anonymous donor!

In the midst of Hans telling this story to Corrie, she said, "Just stop right there." She then called her personal assistant who was upstairs at the time, saying, "Come down and listen to the foolishness of God!" This started a unique relationship between Trans World Radio and Corrie ten Boom, which began with the airing of the first of Corrie's messages on May 14, 1966.

Hans would go to Corrie's home to record the messages. Corrie's involvement in broadcasting over TWR expanded to our station on Bonaire after a visit by Corrie to the Caribbean island, which led to the placing of a burden on her heart to reach the many Dutch-speaking people in The Netherlands Antilles and Suriname. One of her message series was the reading over the air of *The Hiding Place*, the book describing so compellingly her God-blessed life.

Listeners loved her messages. In fact, Hans readily admits to the fact that most of the mail response to the Dutch programs was from Corrie's contributions. Her style was practical and basic, enabling everyone to understand. Corrie's special gift was the ability to include personal illustrations that so clearly depicted the points she was making. Years later, Corrie would still tell of the people she met in her travels who had been so blessed by those "early days" radio programs.

Hans remembered in particular a time when Corrie decided to do a series about the devil. She was to title the messages, "Tricks of the Devil." This decision triggered a series of circumstances which could only be described as an attempt by Satan to avoid the production of these programs. It all started with a serious car accident involving Corrie, just one day before the programs were to be recorded. This ultimately postponed the series for four months. Finally when the recording was underway Hans commented, "Every time we started recording, there would be a banging noise as if someone was working on the central heating system." In fact, this was not the case. However, the interference was so persistent throughout the day that it took an entire afternoon to record only four eight-minute messages. Clearly Corrie had something to say that Satan did not want her to share.

I believe as you read this unique series of Corrie ten Boom's messages, you will quickly recognize the special gift that she brought to the Kingdom, of presenting practical lessons for daily living.

WILLIAM P. MIAL, ASSISTANT TO THE PRESIDENT
FORMER DIRECTOR OF TRANS WORLD RADIO-EUROPE
CARY, NORTH CAROLINA
APRIL 1998

One

A Mirror of God's Glory

And we, who with unveiled faces all reflect the Lord's glory, are being transformed into his likeness with ever-increasing glory, which comes from the Lord, who is the Spirit.

—2 Corinthians 3:18

Have you ever seen a portrait of Sadhu Sundar Singh? That man had such a holy face that I can imagine the Lord Jesus looked like that. He spent much time alone with the Lord in prayer, in meditation, and in fasting. He had visions that give us a picture of heaven. Sadhu Sundar Singh lived according to the Bible. Yes, he was a mirror of the glory of the Lord.

But now I want to speak of you and me, because verse 18 says "we," and that includes you and me. One day we will all share in the nature of the glorified body of Jesus. I can imagine that one of you might say, "Look, I am so worried! Sadhu, yes . . . , but I am so busy. I have six children and no time to be quiet. I can't say that I'm a mirror of the Lord Jesus. I don't look at Him enough." Someone else might say, "I have a very strong ego; I insist on my rights and am easily offended. I feel slighted when people don't greet me. I can't see how I can become like Jesus."

I know, the Bible says, " . . . our citizenship is in heaven. And we eagerly await a Savior from there, the Lord Jesus Christ, who, by the power that enables him to bring everything under his control, will transform our lowly bodies so that they will be like his glorious body" (Phil. 3:20–21). Despite this promise, I understand that someone might confess, "I have a jealous nature. I hide it as much as possible, but I am afraid that it can sometimes be read all over my face. I am afraid that I don't reflect the glory of the Lord." Others might admit, "I like to smoke cigarettes or drink, all very respectably, but I am addicted to it. I don't really feel like a citizen of heaven," or "I like to look good. I think it's wonderful if people appreciate me and think well of me. Being transformed with ever increasing glory would be fine, but taking up that despised cross behind Jesus . . . no, I can't have too much of that."

Well, fill in your confession. You may feel that your character, your circumstances, your experiences are anything but a growing process of being transformed into the likeness of Jesus, continually becoming more and more a mirror of the glory of the Lord. Should we just leave it up to others? To a Sadhu, or to people we know who are further down the road toward sanctification—people who are permanently filled with the Holy Spirit and are such wide-open channels of streams of living water. Yes, if it was up to you and me, I'd agree, "Yes. Let's be level-headed and keep our feet on the ground."

But it doesn't just depend on you and me! I am going to get the answer from the Bible. Read it yourself, then you'll see that it isn't Corrie ten Boom's answer but God's. Philippians 3:20–21 tells us about someone who has the power that enables Him to bring everything under His control.

I once talked to Dr. Elly Beerman-de Roos, an experienced counselor, about a problem that seemed insurmountable to me. "Nothing will come of it," I said. Then she struck her fist on the table and said, "What? He who rose from the dead and rolled away a heavy stone from the grave does not have the power to deal with your problem?" I was ashamed of myself and saw the reality of Jesus' victory. The power which enables Him to bring everything under His control is strong enough for Him to take you and me, who are so busy with our work, by the hand and lead us into silence. " . . . He who began a good work in you will carry it on to completion until the day of Christ Jesus" (Phil. 1:6).

We with our worries, you with your strong ego, and you with your jealous nature, the power that enables Him to bring everything under His control can conquer our sins. Jesus loves sinners! You with your cigarette that is slowly causing lung cancer; you with your drink that makes you a danger when you drive a car; you with your vanity—there is someone who will "keep you strong to the end, so that you will be blameless on the day of our Lord Jesus Christ" (1 Cor. 1:8).

He can do it! What do we have to do? Place our weak hand in His strong hand. Open all the corners, drawers, and rooms of our life for Him so that His victory is not just experienced in one room or in a particular circumstance. No, open all the windows to the light. Don't leave one corner in the dark. Open everything to Him! In 2 Timothy 1:12 we read, " . . . I know whom I have believed, and am convinced that he is able to guard what I have entrusted to him for that day."

Give yourself again or for the first time, but this time completely, to Him of whom it is said in 1 Thessalonians 5:23–24, "May God himself, the God of peace, sanctify you through and through. May your whole spirit, soul and body be kept blameless at the coming of our Lord Jesus Christ. The one who calls you is faithful and he will do it." He will do it through the power that enables Him to bring everything under His control. That counts for us, you and me; for all of us, no exceptions!

"Thank You, Lord Jesus, that Your power is so great that I can do all things through You who gives me strength. Amen."

Two

The Lord's Garden

In the basement of a large tenement house in which many families lived, there was an old broken harp. People had often tried to repair it and play it, but no one had ever succeeded in doing so. One day a beggar came and asked for shelter. The only place for him to spend the night was in a corner of that basement. Late that night people heard the sound of beautiful music coming from the basement. They found the beggar there playing the harp, and they asked, "How were you able to repair the harp and play it so beautifully?" He replied, "I made this harp myself. When I was young, I made lots of harps. This is one of my harps. Shouldn't I be able to repair something I made myself?" John 1:10 says that Jesus "was in the world, and . . . the world was made through him." We have been created by His hands. I despair when I try to change myself and patch myself up. I can't do it and never will be able to do it, but if I surrender myself to Him who made me, I experience miracles!

Charles Spurgeon once said, "What a privilege it is to know that I am a field under heavenly cultivation—not a wilderness but a garden of the Lord, walled by grace, planted according to a divine plan, worked by love, weeded by heavenly discipline, and constantly protected by divine power. A soul, so privileged, is prepared to bring forth fruit to the glory of God." Yes, as Paul says, "You are God's field, God's building" (1 Cor. 3:9). You are a field under heavenly cultivation, walled by grace. We see that grace when we look at the cross of Golgotha. There God's Son bore the sins of the whole world, your sins and mine. But we also see that grace when we look at the empty grave. We have a living Savior, who is with us, who looks at us and loves us, who forgives us if we confess our sins and cleanses us with His blood— what grace! Ephesians 1:7 says of Jesus, "In him we have redemption through his blood, the forgiveness of sins, in accordance with the riches of God's grace...."

We have been planted according to a divine pattern, even if we do not always understand that pattern. God is interested in each of us "microscopically" as well as "telescopically." The hairs of our heads have been counted, but the universe is also in His hand.

Yes, our life is like a garden of the Lord, walled by grace, cultivated by love, and weeded by heavenly discipline. Sin comes between us and God, like the weeds that impede the growth of plants and flowers. Heavenly discipline cultivates us by pulling out the weeds. These can be difficult times in one's life.

I was in a jail cell all alone for four months. That was a time of plowing. I thought, "There'll be nothing left of me." I was desperate, but I suddenly saw God's side of things. I saw myself as a field that was being plowed and weeded. I wrote about this experience in a letter:

"Amazingly I have adapted to this lonely life, together with God. I often speak to my Savior and am gaining more insight into time and eternity. I am prepared to be with Christ in life and in death—that is the best! But life here with Him attracts me too; and I am longing for action. Oh, that continual communion with the Savior—I am thankful that I am alone; me who loves company. I see my sins more clearly, for example my own Ego (with a capital E) and much superficiality.

I once begged for deliverance, but the Lord said, "My grace is sufficient for you." I continue to look to Him and try not to be impatient. I won't be here a moment longer than God thinks is necessary. Pray for me that I will be able to wait for His timing. Life here has wonderful proportions; time is here only to be lived through. It amazes me that I have adapted so well. Some things I can never get used to, but in general I am very happy. It is dark, but then the Savior gives His light and that is wonderful."

My brother was in the same jail during the war and knew what could happen to prisoners there. He came out of jail a sick man and died of that illness a year later. He had the ability to see things from God's perspective, that he was a field under heavenly cultivation. During this time, in which he felt the plowshare and weeding, he wrote in a song that even such hard times can be wonderful because Christ, the Lord, is fighting for His people.

In jail we prisoners lived close to death. When I was in a Nazi concentration camp, I lived for four months in the shadow of a crematorium. There was something liberating about that. You see things in the right proportion because you touch eternity; and then you see everything in the light of eternity. Weeding can hurt. It can wound you, but we are victorious through the blood of the Lamb. We are like clay in the hands of the Potter who shapes, molds, and models us. Don't forget, we are being cultivated and weeded, but our field is constantly under the safe protection of God's omnipotence and His caring love!

The Dutch poet, Bilderdijk once said, "God cares for us with the most exceptional providence."

A soul so prepared is ready to bring forth fruit to the glory of God. What are you? A wilderness or a garden for the Lord? If you are a wilderness, come to Jesus; He will not reject you. He has changed many wildernesses into gardens full of flowers and fruit.

He can make you into a garden under heavenly cultivation, walled by grace, planted according to a divine pattern, tilled by love, weeded by heavenly discipline, and protected by divine omnipotence.

We pray, "Thank You, Lord, that all 'wilderness' people can come to You, and that You don't reject them. You cultivate them to make them into a garden of the Lord, with much fruit and beautiful flowers, by Your Holy Spirit. And the fruit of the Spirit is love, joy, peace, kindness, patience, goodness, faithfulness, gentleness, and self-control. And Lord, then You can use them wonderfully in this 'wilderness' world to feed and empower others. Listen, Lord, to each one who now prays, 'Lord Jesus, my life looks more like a wilderness than a garden. Fill me with Your Holy Spirit so that from now on I can receive power to be a faithful, cheerful witness who bears fruit.' Thank You that in Your Word You say that whoever prays for the Holy Spirit can be sure of receiving Him. Hallelujah! Amen."

Three

Can You Forgive?

*M*atthew 6:14–15 says, "For if you forgive men when they sin against you, your heavenly Father will also forgive you. But if you do not forgive men their sins, your Father will not forgive your sins."

Can you forgive? I can't, but Jesus in me, and Jesus in you, can! Some time ago in America I talked about a great miracle I experienced. When Jesus tells you to love your enemies, He himself gives you that love. I told of how I met a very cruel man in Germany who made my sister suffer a lot when she was dying in a German concentration camp. This man told me the wonderful news that he had found Jesus and had brought all his awful sins to Him. "I know," he said, "that in the Bible it says that Jesus died for the sins of the whole world, for my sins too. When I read 1 John 1:7–9—'The blood of Jesus, his [God's] Son, purifies us from all sin . . . If we confess our sins, he is faithful and just and will forgive us our sins and purify us from all unrighteousness'—I, who had been so terribly cruel, dared to do it. I confessed all my sins and believed that Jesus would purify even my heart by His blood. Then I asked if He would give me the grace to ask one of my victims, who had suffered through my cruelties, for forgiveness."

Then the man asked me, "Fraülein ten Boom, will you forgive me for my cruelties?" I could not do so. It made me bitter to think of what he had done and how my sister Betsie had suffered. Then I prayed, "Lord Jesus, thank You for Romans 5:5 [about how God has poured out His love into our hearts by the Holy Spirit]; thank You that God's love takes away my bitterness." Then a miracle happened. It was as if I felt God's love flowing through my arm. I was able to forgive that man and even shake his hand. You never experience God's love more marvelously than at the moment He gives you love for your enemies.

In America, a lady approached me after I had spoken about this text. She handed me a key. "Will you please destroy this?" she asked. "Yes, but why?" She said, "It's the key to the home of a lady who stole the love of my husband." I do not know what her plans were—maybe to burst in on him and that woman, maybe to catch them red-handed, perhaps to take revenge. I know what happened when she gave me that key. She had forgiven them, and the Lord Jesus had performed the miracle of replacing hatred in her heart with God's love.

Recently, I have met many young people. Many of them had dreadful pasts—addiction to drugs, crime. I sometimes asked them, "Have you asked your parents to forgive you for the pain that you caused them in the past?" I also found that they themselves had to forgive. "Have you forgiven your parents for the bad things they did in your life?" I saw great deliverance when, in God's power, they straightened out problems between them and their parents and put away their bitterness and lack of forgiveness. It was wonderful to see how many young people were able to forgive and ask for forgiveness by the power of the Holy Spirit.

Such a shadow in our lives can keep us in bondage and make us so unhappy. Jesus came like a light in the darkness so that everyone who believes in Him will not remain in darkness. Is there the darkness of bitterness or guilt in your life? I would like to give you some advice: Straighten things out today! Ask for forgiveness and tell those who have hurt you that you have forgiven them too. Do it together with Jesus. He will do it. He is the Victor, and He makes you and me conquerors. The Lord Jesus will cause you to be a great blessing to those with whom you have not been able to get along.

Not only young people who do not know the Lord need this truth. Those of you who have known the Lord for a long time and have unforgiveness in your hearts: Come to Him and pray with me:

"Lord, will You show me if there is anything between You and me, between me and someone else, me and my parents, me and my children? Will You help me when I ask them for forgiveness and when I forgive them? Thank You for Your strong love because You said in Romans 5:5, 'God has poured out his love into our hearts by the Holy Spirit, whom he has given us.' Lord, I give everything to You—my past, my present, my future, my bitterness, everything. Thank You that You in me are the Victor! Amen."

Four

God's Answer to Worry

1/7/2000

oday I am going to talk about worry and anxiety. My message is for Christians, but even if you are not a Christian, still listen because you will hear something of the richness that you inherit when you become a Christian! The path is open. Don't you realize that yet? He died on the cross for the sins of the whole world, for your sins. You can do it now—come to Jesus. The Bible says that whoever comes to Him will never be turned away. Believe in Him, and He will make you a child of God. That is the way to become a Christian.

When you become a Christian, the Lord will train you with great love. You see, being a Christian does not mean that you won't need to fight any battles. You are now a strategic target for the enemy. One of the most successful weapons of the devil is worry. To be a conqueror in that battle, you have to learn to listen to what the Bible says about fighting the enemy. I will talk about that and also share my experiences and those of other Christians. God speaks through His Word, but also through His children.

I once read that the lifestyle of a Christian should be one of victory, joy, and abundance. From our side, we require only a dose of need and openness to accept help from the Lord. The doors of heaven are open; so if I hold on to feelings that prevent me from living under an open heaven, then it is no wonder I feel depressed. I read these words when I was extremely miserable, and I was ashamed. I picked up my Bible and read Philippians 4:6–7: "Do not be anxious about anything, but in everything, by prayer and petition, with thanksgiving, present your requests to God. And the peace of God, which transcends all understanding, will guard your hearts and your minds in Christ Jesus." Suddenly I saw what the Lord meant. As children of the light, we have to live as people who are powerful, content, calm, and free. That is the task. The Bible says that the joy of the Lord will be our strength.

There is something else very practical: We have to take good note of the blessings He gives and has given. We can learn to count our blessings. The Bible says, "Do not be anxious about anything, but in everything, by prayer and petition, with thanksgiving, present your requests to God" (Phil. 4:6). Yes, that means prayer. Have you ever been discouraged about prayer? Worry is very frequently being concerned for others, and often, it can take a long time before you notice any response to prayer for others.

Some time ago, I had a wonderful experience. In a television broadcast with Willem Duys, a Dutch TV personality, I had a wonderful opportunity to share the Gospel with Dutch people. It was on Easter Sunday, in the evening. I was told that I may have given my Easter message to as many as six million people. Many people responded. I received phone calls, letters, and visits, and was able to do a lot of wonderful pastoral work. I was very encouraged.

I have experienced answers to prayer for more than seventy years. When I was five years old, I asked the Lord Jesus to come into my heart. He did so, and He has never forsaken me. I immediately became very concerned for people. Behind the Barteljorisstraat, where I lived, was the Smedestraat, where there were many bars. I saw many drunk people on the streets who were taken to the police station in the Smedestraat. I decided to do something about what I saw. I began to end every prayer with these words: "And Lord Jesus, will You save and convert the people in the Smedestraat?" After the television program, I received a letter from a woman who wrote, "My husband was so happy to hear that you were born in Haarlem. He lived in the Smedestraat for seventeen years and worked at the police station. He and I know the Lord Jesus too." An answer after seventy-three years.

I always went to Christian schools, but when I was fifteen years old, I went to a non-Christian school. I was there with pupils and teachers who did not know the Lord. How I talked to them, and moreover . . . how I prayed for them. Recently, I received a letter: "Do you know, Corrie, that sixty years ago we were at school together? I saw you on TV. I'd like to tell you that I am a follower of Jesus too." An answer after sixty years.

Another man phoned me: "Do you know that forty-five years ago you said the same thing to me as you said on TV? I always refused to do what you advised: Accept Jesus as my Savior. Now I believe I have to say 'yes' to Him. May I come and see you?" I replied, "Come quickly!" I prayed with him and said, "Ask the Lord Jesus to come into your heart." And he prayed, "Jesus, I can't get my heart open. Will you break the door down?" Jesus began a miracle in his life—an answer after forty-five years.

I also received a letter from a man who wrote these words: "Twenty-five years ago I came out of a concentration camp into the house that you had opened for ex-prisoners. You presented the Gospel to me, but I was not ready for it. I saw you on television, and I can now write to tell you that I have found the Lord"—an answer after twenty-five years.

Why am I telling you all this? So that you see how God's work is sometimes slow, but very sure. Don't be discouraged in your intercession for your son, husband, wife, daughter, or your neighbor, friend, or whoever you are concerned about. The devil will say to you, "Stop—you can surely see that God is not answering you." But the devil is a liar. Keep it up! I believe that when we get to heaven, we will see that not one prayer of intercession was lost. I have shared with you something of the joy of heaven in all those answers after so many years. Yes, the Bible says, "Cast your bread upon the waters, for after many days you will find it again" (Eccl. 11:1).

Shall we pray? "Thank You, Lord, that we can and must make our needs known to You through prayer and thanksgiving. You always listen, hear, and answer in Your time. Will You, by Your Holy Spirit, fill our hearts with faith instead of doubt? Thank You, Lord. Amen."

Five

1/13/2000

Worrying Is Disobedient

Worrying is stupid. The Bible says, "Do not worry about anything." If you are worrying, you are being disobedient. I had to understand that before I could stop doing it. First, I tried in my own strength—positive thinking, not fretting anymore. That approach was about as successful as attacking a lion with a toy pistol! Only the Lord can set you free through the Holy Spirit. Ask for forgiveness. Be cleansed by the blood of the Lord Jesus and be filled by the Spirit, of whom Paul says, "God did not give us a spirit of timidity, but a spirit of power, of love and of self-discipline" (2 Tim. 1:7).

If the Bible is true—and it is true!—fear, worrying, and anxiety actually question the trustworthiness of God. Then apparently we are saying, "God, you are not speaking the truth." In other words, "You are lying." Will we believe what the Lord tells us in Philippians 4:19—"My God will meet all your needs according to his glorious riches in Christ Jesus"—and in Hebrews 13:5—"... never will I leave you; never will I forsake you?" These promises allow us to say with confidence, "The Lord is my helper, I will not fear; what can man do to me?"

First Peter 5:7 says, "Cast all your anxiety on him because he cares for you," and Matthew 6:31–34 says, "So do not worry, saying, 'What shall we eat?' or 'What shall we drink?' or 'What shall we wear?' For the pagans run after all these things, and your heavenly Father knows that you need them. But seek first his kingdom and his righteousness, and all these things will be given to you as well. Therefore do not worry about tomorrow, for tomorrow will worry about itself. Each day has enough trouble of its own."

It was liberating when I understood that fear and worry are sin. No book in the world has such a wonderful answer to our problem of sin as does the Bible: Confess, let yourself be cleansed, and allow the Holy Spirit to control your heart, because the fruit of the Spirit is precisely the opposite of our sin. Galatians 5:22 says that the fruit of the Spirit is "love, joy, peace, patience, kindness, goodness, faithfulness, gentleness, and self-control."

The Lord Jesus gives a clear comparison in John 15. We are the branches, Jesus is the vine. Abiding—remaining—in Him is the secret. Jesus does the work of bearing fruit—Jesus, who bore our sins on the cross; Jesus, who is alive and whose Spirit lives in us; Jesus, the conqueror who makes us more than conquerors. I am weak; the devil is strong, but Jesus is much stronger than the devil. Therefore, Jesus and I together are much stronger than the devil, much stronger than the demon of worry.

Once, I had a burden that weighed heavily on me. I set it down and looked at it. Then I saw that everything about my burden was borrowed. One part belonged to the following day, one part to the next week. My burden was a huge, stupid mistake. I realized that worrying is carrying tomorrow's burden with today's strength. It's carrying two days at once. It's prematurely thinking of tomorrow. On the calendar, there is only one day for action, and that is today.

Making plans is time-consuming. Time is necessary for making wise plans, but carrying them out belongs to only one day—today. We become concerned about the future—our financial concerns, our health. Where does this lead to? Nowhere. Nowhere that is worth the trouble because tension ruins things. It depletes the energy that you need to live today. The Holy Spirit does not give you a clear blueprint for your life, but He leads you from moment to moment. Live for today! The sun will shine tomorrow on the problems that tomorrow brings.

I read somewhere, "Why don't we look for something that is easier than anxiety? Worried people are like tightrope walkers, trying to walk over a rope from the past to the future, balancing between hope and fear. In one hand they hold a bag with the disordered past, in the other a bag, the feared future. Worrying does not take away tomorrow's grief; it takes away today's strength. It does not enable us to avoid evil, but it makes us incapable of dealing with it when it comes."

I once heard a nice story, a kind of legend. A small clock, which had just been finished by its maker, was put on a shelf in his shop between two old clocks that were busily and loudly ticking away the seconds. "So," said one of the old clocks to the newcomer, "you've just started this task. I feel sorry for you. You are bravely ticking now, but you'll be very tired once you've ticked thirty-three million times."

"Thirty-three million ticks?" said the startled clock, "but I could never do that!" He immediately stopped in desperation.

"Come on, stupid," said the other clock. "Why do you listen to such talk? That's not how things are. At each moment you only need to tick once. Isn't that easy? And then again. That's just as easy. Carry on like that."

"Oh, if that's all," the new clock cried, "then that's easy enough. Off I go." And he began again to bravely tick each moment, without paying attention to the months and the millions of ticks. When the year was up, he had ticked thirty-three million times without realizing it.

Yes, living for the moment, that's what you need. The Lord's prayer says, "Give us today our daily bread." Deuteronomy 33:25 says, " . . . your strength will equal your days." That is a promise made more than three thousand years ago. A person does not fall so much because of the troubles of one day, but if tomorrow's burden is added, this load can become very, very heavy. It is wonderfully easy to live just for the day.

Shall we pray? "Lord Jesus, please teach us by Your Holy Spirit in us to live for today. Thank You that You forgive us if we ask forgiveness for the sin of worry, and that You set us free. Thank You that we know You are the Victor. Amen."

Six

The Miracle of Prayer
Is the Answer to Our Anxiety

If you accept the Lord Jesus, you are a child of God. Immediately, however, you also enter a battle, because the devil wants to entice you away from victorious life with Jesus. He tries to frighten you. But, fortunately, the Lord Jesus wants to fill your heart with His Holy Spirit, who gives us God's love (Rom. 5:5). Yes, God's love is poured out in our hearts by the Holy Spirit, and this love conquers fear and worry. When the Lord says in Isaiah 41:10, "Do not fear," He gives us the reason why that is possible. He says, "So do not fear, for I am with you; do not be dismayed, for I am your God. I will strengthen you and help you; I will uphold you with my righteous right hand." Are you sure that you are God's child? No? Then you must speak to the Lord Jesus today and ask Him into your heart, because then He will make you a child of God.

I want to speak again about worry and anxiety, and what that means to you if you are a child of God. Listen to what the Lord Jesus says in the Sermon on the Mount: "Therefore do not worry about tomorrow, for tomorrow will worry about itself. Each day has enough trouble of its own" (Matt. 6:34).

If you accept the Lord Jesus and follow Him, He will do a miracle in your life: the miracle of being born again. That means that to those who accept Jesus, He gives the right to become children of God. We are born into God's family, and we grow like children. One of the experiences of growth is that you accept the promises in the Bible and you obey the commandments that are so clearly stated in it. One of those commandments that gives such comfort is Matthew 6:34: " . . . do not worry about tomorrow." Through faith you have become a child of God, you have been saved, and through faith you also achieve victory over worry, fear, and other sins. Cast your burdens on the Lord. You do that when you pray.

Yes, prayer is so important. If possible, look for a place where you can be alone with the Lord and tell Him what you need. Pour your heart out to Him. Fine language is not necessary. If you are suffering from a nervous stomach, don't just ask the Lord to take away the stomach complaint, but tell Him what makes you nervous and pray about that. Pray specifically and expect a specific answer. If you ask God for bread, He will not give you a stone. If God does not answer right away, then go to Him again. Be thankful that you have a reason to go to Him again. Study the prayers in the Bible. They are not formal. They are spoken in ordinary language. Approach God as you would your mother, your father, a friend. Tell Him about your concerns; tell Him that you have sinned by worrying. Tell Him that you want victory over your anxiety. Make a clear choice. Believe in the Lord. It is not your prayer, but your Savior, who is the answer!

If you do not pray specifically, you trust more in the prayer than in the Lord. At least, it can be that way. Prayer is a family business, a child speaking to His Father. Prayer opens the door to Him who can and will save you from your worries. God's power is shown in our weakness. Galatians 1:16 says that Paul did not consult flesh and blood. Consulting people about your fears and worries—instead of bringing them to the Lord in prayer—can make them even bigger and heavier. Prayer is not meant to be one-way traffic. Imagine that someone comes in and asks you a question but then immediately turns around and leaves without waiting for an answer! We have to take time to speak with the Lord and to listen to His answer. We have to practice God's hidden companionship. Paul says in 2 Corinthians 10:5 that we have to take captive every thought to make it obedient to Christ. We have to do that, too, with our worries.

As well as prayer—the companionship of the Lord in your quiet time—there is another wonderful experience we can have: praying together. Praying together is extremely important. The Lord says that where two or three are gathered together in His name, there He is in the midst of them. The devil tries to hinder praying together in all kinds of ways.

I know of a small group of boys and girls in America who met together in the mornings to pray. They had seen lots of things go wrong at school. They soon noticed that the atmosphere in their class improved greatly after they had prayed. More and more young Christians joined them. After a time, they were forbidden to use the room. They looked for a quiet place where they could pray and found a cemetery near the school.

Winter came. They were very cold at the cemetery, but they carried on. One day the principal saw the students coming from the cemetery, and he asked them what they were doing there. They said that the cemetery was the only quiet place they could find where they could pray undisturbed. The principal was so touched that he opened a pleasant room for them where they could hold their prayer meeting each day. And that continues regularly. Miracles happen in that school. Instead of constant arguments between teachers and pupils, there is an atmosphere of unity. The principal told me this and said that he was sure this was the answer to the boys' and girls' prayers.

Shall we pray together? "Lord Jesus, how wonderful that You are a friend who understands our problems, and that we can tell You everything. Give us the opportunity to seek You and to find You by praying with others. Thank You that You gave us the promise: where two or three are gathered together in Your name, You are in the midst of them. Thank You. Amen."

Seven

Does God Answer Prayer?

Today I am speaking again to God's children. It is so wonderful to be a child of God. Listener, are you still not a child of God? Come to Jesus. He gives us the right to become a child of God. He did everything necessary for us to call God "Father." He did that when He carried our punishment on the Cross. Jesus is alive. He is with you. Speak to Him; He can hear you. Place your hand in His, and then He will make you a child of the King—God's child.

I want to talk to God's children about answered prayer. Years ago I spoke in Japan about the answer to our problem of worrying. I asked this question: "Do you know the feeling of worrying—feeling as if your heart was like a suitcase, heavy with your burdens?" I lifted up my suitcase and let them see how full it was with heavy objects. I told them that my heart felt like that last week. I read to them this glorious text: "Cast all your anxiety on him because he cares for you" (1 Peter 5:7). Then I took two objects out of the suitcase and laid them on the table. I said, "Here is the trip I am taking next week to a town where I don't know anyone. Will You give me strength and guidance? Will You lead me to Christians in that town who can show me the way around?" I took another object from my suitcase and laid it on the table, and I continued, "These are my friends at home. They wrote to me and told me that they had been in a car accident. Will You heal those who were injured? Here is the boy who refused to give his heart to You yesterday. Will You touch his heart?" As I named each concern, I took an object out of my case. After I unpacked everything, I said, "Amen." That's prayer. That's good.

But what I did after my "Amen" was not good! I packed all the objects on the table back into my suitcase. I explained that that's exactly what we do if we take our concerns to the Lord and then let those worries enter our hearts again. We must bring our burdens to Jesus and leave them there!

Fourteen years later, at an evangelistic conference, I met a Japanese man. He said, "Corrie ten Boom, when I see you, I think of your suitcase full of worries. I saw you that day when you unpacked your suitcase and then repacked the objects back into your suitcase. That experience taught me how to pray." A visible illustration stays in the memory for a long time.

Now I ask you: Have you unpacked your case of worries in your morning prayers? Good—your heavenly Father knows what you need. He who cares for a sparrow also cares for you (Matt. 10:29). But what did you do after you prayed? Is your heart just as heavy as before you prayed? Ask for forgiveness for your disbelief, and ask the Lord if, through His Holy Spirit, He will teach you how to pray and teach you to unpack your case of worries. He cultivates faith and trust in your heart. He will also show you that nothing is too big for His omnipotence or too small for His love.

There are people who trust the Lord for their eternal salvation but not for the worries of every day. They do not see that our problems are the material God intends to use to build a miracle. God loves you! Imagine a little girl going to her father with a broken doll. The little one is crying with grief. What does the father do? Does he say, "That old doll's not worth a cent, throw it away?" Of course not. He takes the doll and tries to repair it. Why does a grown man take such an old doll seriously? Because he sees it through the eyes of that little girl, whom he loves so much. Your heavenly Father sees your problem through your eyes because He loves you.

I like to tell of an experience I had when I was in prison. I had a cold and did not have a handkerchief. I told my sister Betsie, and she said, "Pray for a handkerchief." I started to laugh. Betsie prayed, "Father, I pray in Jesus' name that you will give Corrie a handkerchief because she has a cold." Just a bit later, I heard my name being called. I went to the window and saw a friend of mine who was also a prisoner and who worked in the hospital. "Here," she said, "take this, I am bringing you a present." I opened the package. It was a handkerchief! "How did you know that I needed a handkerchief? Did you know I had a cold?" "No," she said, "I was sewing handkerchiefs from an old piece of sheet, and a voice in my heart said, 'Take a handkerchief to Corrie ten Boom.'"

Can you understand what a handkerchief meant to me at that moment? That handkerchief, made of an old piece of sheet, was a message from heaven for me. It told me that there was a heavenly Father who listens when one of His children on planet earth prays for an impossibly small thing—a handkerchief. That same heavenly Father says to one of His other children, "Take a handkerchief to Corrie ten Boom." Isn't that wonderful? That is something Paul calls "the foolishness of

God," which is so much wiser than the wisdom of man. Read about it in 1 Corinthians 1–2.

Does God answer our prayers? Often, but not always. Why? Because He knows what we don't know. He knows everything. When we get to heaven, we'll thank God for all the answered prayers, but it may be that we will thank Him for the unanswered prayers even more because, then, we will be able to see things from God's perspective. We will see that God never makes mistakes.

Shall we pray? "Thank You, Father, that You love us so much and that we, if we are Your children, will one day see that. Will You teach us through Your Holy Spirit to bring our worries to You and leave them with You? Give us great faith to accept unanswered prayers and see that nothing can separate us from Your ocean of love in Christ Jesus our Lord. Hallelujah. Amen."

Eight

Are Unanswered Prayers God's Mistakes?

J am going to tell you something about so-called unanswered prayers. First of all, unanswered prayers are not evidence that God makes mistakes but, rather, that God knows what we do not know. God knows everything. I was in a concentration camp with my sister Betsie, and she became very sick. I took her to a hospital in the camp, and when she was in bed she said, "Will you pray with me for the Lord to heal me? Corrie, the Lord Jesus said, 'In My name you can lay on hands and they will be healed.' Will you do that?"

I prayed for her. We both believed that Betsie would be healed. The next morning I looked through the hospital window and saw them lifting Betsie's dead body from the bed to take it to the crematorium. That was the darkest hour of my life.

A couple of days later, I was unexpectedly released, probably because of a human error, but definitely through one of God's miracles. When I got to the office to sign out, I realized that they didn't know that Betsie was dead. It occurred to me to find out what would have happened to Betsie if she had not died. I asked, "Is my sister being released too?" The answer was,

"No, she is staying here for the duration of the war." "Can I stay with her?" I asked. The man became furious. "Get out, you are leaving immediately," he ordered.

Immediately, I saw God's perspective of the events. Just imagine that Betsie had gotten better and that I had had to leave her in that terrible camp and go to Holland alone.... I praised God and thanked Him for that unanswered prayer. I knew that Betsie was now in her Father's house with its many mansions. I knew that she couldn't be happier and that life couldn't be more glorious for her.

I therefore dare to expect that one day we will praise God and thank Him for all answered prayers, but even more so for the so-called unanswered prayers. A wise mother and father do not give their children everything they ask for. They know, better than the children, what is good for each child. This is not always understood. In countries in which communism reigns, Christians are often persecuted. When I told those Christians that Christians in Holland were faithfully praying for them, they were very appreciative, but not one person ever asked me, "Will you ask our brothers and sisters in Holland to pray that the persecution here will cease?" No, the request was always, "Will you ask them to pray that God will give us strength and courage to endure persecution?" May I ask you to faithfully pray for your brothers and sisters who are living in countries where they are persecuted and oppressed?

What does Paul say about prayer, both answered and unanswered? The text in Philippians is very clear: "Do not be anxious about anything, but in everything, by prayer and petition, with thanksgiving, present your requests to God" (4:6). "And my God will meet all your needs according to his glorious riches in Christ Jesus" (4:19). Did Paul experience that? Yes. But in verse 12 he writes, "I know what it is to be in need, and I know what it is to have plenty." He surely must have begged God for food when he was hungry, but he accepted unanswered prayer with this attitude: "I can do everything through him who gives me strength" (4:13). If you bring your requests to God through prayer and supplication, "The peace of God, which transcends all understanding, will guard your hearts and your minds in Christ Jesus" (4:7). The Holy Spirit allowed Paul to see circumstances from God's perspective.

Paul speaks about persecution, hardship, and famine in Romans 8:35–39. Nothing can separate us from the love of Christ? No! In all these things we are more than conquerors through Him who loved us. Nothing can separate us from the love of God that is in Christ Jesus our Lord. If something extremely serious happens, we can be confident that the best, the very best, is yet to come!

In New Zealand I met a boy, Chris L., who had so seriously injured his neck in an accident that he was almost completely paralyzed. Fortunately, his brain was not damaged. He was able to read and type, and had helped me correct a book that I had written. We became good friends. I perceived, however, that he could not accept that the Lord might not heal him. I spoke a lot to him and prayed with him so that he would surrender his suffering to God. I slept in the room next to his because he often needed help during the night. One night I could hear that he was awake, and I knew that there was a battle going on in his heart. I heard him cry out, "Oh God, make me willing to surrender everything to You!" The next morning I saw an expression of great joy and peace on his face. Chris has now become an assistant pastor, and I know he is a blessing to many.

Jesus' death on the cross seemed to be a total fiasco, but there He fulfilled everything necessary to save and redeem you and me. He carried our sins and pain. That is why it is possible for us to bring our so-called unanswered prayers to Him and to surrender them into the hands of Him who carried our problems and unanswered prayers on the cross. Yes, hallelujah, Jesus carried our pain, and His work is complete.

Shall we pray? "Thank You, Lord Jesus, that You have brought us to the ocean of God's love and that nothing can separate us from it. Thank You that Your Holy Spirit allows us to see circumstances from Your perspective so that we do not need to fear, even if the earth were to give way and the mountains were to move into the heart of the sea, as the psalmist says. Hallelujah. What a Savior! Amen."

Nine

Intercession

1/15/2000

It is wonderful to be called to be intercessors. Anyone can do it! Do you know that not one of your prayers for someone else is lost? Not a single one. We sometimes forget that. The devil laughs at our plans. He smiles if we are up to our ears in work, but he trembles when we pray.

When I was five, I asked the Lord Jesus into my heart. The Lord made me an intercessor immediately!

First Timothy 2:1–3 says, "I urge, then, first of all, that requests, prayers, intercession and thanksgiving be made for everyone—for kings and all those in authority, that we may live peaceful and quiet lives in all godliness and holiness. This is good, and pleases God our Savior, who wants all men to be saved and to come to a knowledge of the truth."

Intercession is important work. Do you know that Isaiah 59:16 says that God was amazed that there was no intercessor? I remember that my sister Betsie and I were once in a Dutch concentration camp in Vught. We were there because we had rescued Jews. One day we thought that we were being called to be released, but, instead, we found ourselves standing in the middle of the concentration camp in front of a bunker that was being used as the jail. Standing to our right and left were prisoners. As we stood there, we realized that we might all be killed.

Suddenly, we noticed that there were no longer any guards. One of the prisoners shouted out, "Is there anyone here who can pray?" Betsie answered, "Yes, I can pray and I will." And she prayed! She prayed for herself, she prayed for the men next to her, she prayed for me, and she thanked the Lord that, even if we were killed, the best was yet to come for those who belonged to the Lord Jesus. She asked the Lord to take our hand if we were about to pass through the valley of the shadow of death. I can't remember what else she prayed, but it was a wonderful prayer. How marvelous it is to intercede.

Some time ago I was in Cuba with my assistant, Ellen de Kroon. It was difficult to work there; sometimes it was even very dangerous. Once I prayed, "Oh Lord, please tell our friends in Holland to pray for us." I do that quite often, and it is just as if I am sending them a telegram via headquarters: heaven. I feel so safe because I know my friends are praying for me.

When I returned to Holland, a girl came up to me—a very simple girl, not intellectual—but she loved the Lord Jesus very much. She approached me and said, "Auntie, on the 10th of April, you were in danger, weren't you?" I asked, "What makes you say that?" She said, "I woke up in the middle of the night, and the Lord said to me, 'Will you pray for Corrie?' And I did." That was precisely the moment I had asked for prayer! And you know, for that girl it was just as wonderful.

If you are an intercessor, you are in direct contact with the Lord. You are in the service of the King of kings. A while ago, I spoke in a large Australian church about the wonderful text of Revelation 3:20, in which the Lord Jesus says, "Here I am! I stand at the door and knock. If anyone hears my voice and opens the door, I will come in . . ." The Lord Jesus is speaking not only to people who know Him and love Him, but also to people who do not know Him or love Him. When He knocks, He listens to see if we say, "Yes." Even if we know Him, we often have to say, "Yes, Lord Jesus, come in." Do you know that the people in Laodicea to whom the Lord was speaking were Christians? They went to church, but something was missing: Jesus stood outside the door of their hearts.

I spoke to the people there in Australia and said, "It is so glorious that everybody may know that Jesus is knocking at the door of your heart. If you say, 'Yes,' He will come in." Afterwards I gave a kind of invitation: "If you said, 'Yes,' for the first time to the Lord Jesus, come up to the front and go to the room behind me. We'll pray for you there, give you some literature and explain to you what it means to have asked the Lord Jesus into your heart for the first time."

The first to come were two small girls. One of them asked me, "Am I too small to ask Jesus to come into my heart?" I said, "Why no, you're not too small. I was five when I asked the Lord into my heart, and He came—and He has never, ever deserted me. He has always stayed. That's a long time ago. The Lord Jesus is even interested in sparrows, and you are much bigger than a sparrow." Then the little girl said, "Lord Jesus, I have been very naughty, but will You please come into my heart and make it clean, cleanse it completely with Your blood. Amen."

Oh, it was so marvelous. Everyone heard what the little girl said. I am sure that the Lord came, just as He will come into your heart if you say, "Yes." I said to the other little one, "Would you like to do it, too?" She said, "I already did, a fortnight ago, and since then I've been praying for Mary every day, and now Mary did it." I said, "Then you must pray together for a third girl."

They looked at each other and at the same moment, they both said, "Anna." I said, "Then Anna it must be." They promised to pray for Anna, and when Anna had asked the Lord Jesus into her heart, then they could pray together for a fourth girl.

Intercession entered the hearts of the two little girls. Intercession can begin in your heart too. Surely you know someone who does not know the Lord. Pray for them and share the Gospel with him or her. Keep praying, and if the other person says, "Yes," pray together for a third person. Intercession can be the salvation of many people. Oh, if everyone would do it now, there would be a great revival in many countries.

Shall we pray? "Lord, will You use me? Will You use me as an intercessor? Thank You that I may intercede for others! Will You start a chain reaction of intercession in my heart, so that I can pray for another person, and then we can pray together for a third person, and then the three of us can pray for a fourth person? Thank You, Lord, that You want to use me! Hallelujah! Amen."

Ten

How Do We Prepare
for Jesus' Return?

I laid down my worries and looked at them. Part of them, I noticed, belonged to the past and another part to the future. Then I read in the Bible, "Each day has enough trouble of its own" (Matt. 6:34).

In my book about my life called *The Hiding Place*, I tell about an experience I had as a little girl. It was the first time I had seen a dead child. I had never encountered death before, and I became terribly worried—not just about my own death, but also that those whom I loved might die. I told my father about my fears. "Daddy, I am afraid that I will never be brave and strong enough to be a martyr for Jesus." He asked me, "If you go on a train journey from Haarlem to Amsterdam, when do I give you the ticket, three weeks ahead of time?" "No, Daddy, the day I am traveling," I replied.

"Right," said father, "and that's what God does too. You don't need a ticket now. You don't need the strength yet to suffer persecution for Jesus or to bear the death of people you love. But when the time comes, the Lord will give you the ticket right on time, all the strength and grace and courage you need." That comforted me very much, and often if I am worrying about the future, I think of my father's illustration and say to myself, "No, God has not given me the ticket yet, but I don't need it right now!"

Everyone who pays attention to world events, which we understand as signs of the time that Jesus may return very soon, can almost become scared at what the Bible says about the time of the Antichrist and the terrible things that will happen then. The moment will also come when we must all stand before a righteous God.

To be prepared, we need many promises that are in the Bible. We have to absorb them. Do you understand what I mean? Every promise of God's in the Bible is in Jesus. "Yes and Amen." And I notice—and I believe this is very clear in the Bible—that the Lord Jesus Himself wants to make us ready for that great day, when we will see Him face to face. I am so much looking forward to His return, aren't you?

Why do we look forward to it? Because we love Him. But He loves us much more than we love Him. That's why I believe that He is looking forward to it much more than we are! We understand that we have to be ready upon His return—completely ready. Whoever has this hope cleanses himself, as He is clean.

But then so often we try and we fail. It doesn't work. Even if I do my utmost to be pure and holy, and to walk in a good relationship with God and people, I still experience the temptations of the enemy. I think the enemy is very active at the moment in attacking God's children. He knows that time is very short.

How can you and I be prepared? Not by trying and trying again; that can be a victory for devout people who live by the flesh. They think they are so good—a great victory for the devil. But the answer to being prepared is this: Surrender yourself to

Him who wants you so much and who is prepared to make you ready for His return. First Thessalonians 3:12 says, "May the Lord make your love increase and overflow for each other and for everyone else, just as ours does for you."

Jesus doesn't only want to save us from our sins, but He wants to restore the image of God in us. We cannot summon up that love, but that's not necessary either. If we place our weak hand in the strong hand of the Lord, then He does it. He himself makes His love abundant. The Bible also says, "May he strengthen your hearts so that you will be blameless and holy in the presence of our God and Father when our Lord Jesus comes with all his holy ones" (1 Thess. 3:13).

"Blameless and holy." No, we cannot do that, we cannot become like that by trying, but He can do it! First Thessalonians 5:23 says, "May God himself, the God of peace, sanctify you through and through. May your whole spirit, soul and body be kept blameless at the coming of our Lord Jesus Christ."

How can that be? Blameless! Holy! Such words can just make us frightened when we look at ourselves. But, if we look to the Lord, we have no need to be afraid because the last part of this text is, "The one who calls you is faithful and he will do it." What will He do? He will give you and me the ticket we need for our journey.

What is that ticket? Not until then shall we fully understand (we understand it just a little bit now) that on the cross at Golgotha, Jesus fulfilled everything that was needed to prepare us for the future. Jesus said, "It is finished." If we look to the cross at Golgotha then we know: He is faithful, who did it and will do it. It is He who calls us. What you and I have to do is place our weak hand in His strong hand, surrender to Him, and then walk with Him through life. He wants to hold on to our hand with strength and accompany us on the narrow path. Do you know that wonderful song? We ourselves are weak, but in Him we are strong. In Him, who said that He will make us more than conquerors. So we need not fear the future. He will accompany us on the narrow path.

"Thank You, Lord, that we do not need to worry, but that You will guide us, even in these very difficult times. And not only that, Lord, You want to make us Your witnesses in a world in which there is so much darkness. Will You make us the light of the world? Thank You, Lord. Amen."

Eleven

God Prepares Us

What a world we live in! I find the news broadcasts so terrible that reading newspapers and listening to the news can make me despondent and sometimes almost desperate. We cannot see the final outcome, and often we become frightened as to where all this bad news will lead.

What a comfort it is to read the Bible and to see that God has long known what is happening now and that He has promised us a wonderful future in spite of all these terrible events that are occurring. In His words of farewell in Luke 21, the Lord Jesus described what we are now reading about in the newspapers.

That puzzling book, the Revelation of John, is much easier to understand now than it was ten or twenty years ago. There are terrible things prophesied in that book, but John saw the divine perspective. In Revelation 21:4 he says, "He will wipe every tear from their eyes. There will be no more death or mourning or crying or pain, for the old order of things has passed away." If we read the news reports we say, "The worst is yet to come." If we read the Bible we can cry out, "The best is still to come!" Jesus promised, "I am coming," and "I make all things new." Then this world, this dark world, will be covered with the knowledge of the Lord as the waters cover the sea.

If you read God's blueprint of world history, you are secure in the knowledge that God has plans for this world, and not problems. There has never been panic in heaven! The Lord Jesus said to watch out for the signs of the times. If we do that, then we know that He will return soon.

How can we be prepared? By surrendering to Him, of whom Paul said in Philippians 1:6, "I . . . being confident of this, that he who began a good work in you will carry it on to completion until the day of Christ Jesus." Here we see that on our side it is not a battle, not striving, not struggling, but surrendering.

The Lord Jesus wants to prepare us for His return. He loves us. He desires us more than we long for Him. In 1 Thessalonians 5:23–24 we read, "May God himself, the God of peace, sanctify you through and through. May your whole spirit, soul, and body be kept blameless at the coming of our Lord Jesus Christ. The one who calls you is faithful and he will do it." Just think what that means: you and I, blameless in spirit, soul, and body. That is possible because He who calls you is faithful. He will do it! Place your weak hand in His strong hand. He is faithful and He will do it.

Shall we pray? "Thank You, Lord Jesus, that You want to prepare us for Your return. Thank You that You have so clearly shown us the blueprint for world events in Your Word and that we know that if we, the branches, are connected to the vine, that in these difficult times we can produce fruits of peace, love, and comfort. Hold us tight. Amen."

Twelve

God Comforts Us

At the moment it is very dark in our world. The Lord Jesus told us that if we belong to Him, we are the light of the world. How much that is needed now!

Is that possible in a time like this? Yes, it is possible. I have experienced it myself. There was a time in my life when it was so dark that I said, "It has never been so bad and it can't get any worse." I was weak, and there was bitterness and fear in my heart instead of light. I had known the Lord Jesus for a long time, and I knew that I could find shelter with Him. I was with my sister, Betsie, in jail, prisoners of people who had been trained in cruelty. Everything was dark and awful.

Then Betsie and I started talking about the Lord Jesus. We opened the Bible and read about the ocean of God's love, into which we could throw ourselves—completely into His loving arms. We read what Jesus said before He left, "My peace I give you" (John 14:27). We felt His love and peace, and we sang softly, "Safe in the Arms of Jesus." We were so happy, and that evening Betsie said, "Wasn't it a wonderful day? We learned so much from the Lord."

How had we experienced that, how had we come to that? We did what Jesus said: "Come to me, all you who are weary and burdened, and I will give you rest" (Matt 11:28). Jesus gave us rest and a happiness that passes beyond all understanding.

Paul had many miserable experiences of cruelty and imprisonment. He wrote in 2 Corinthians 1:3–4, "Praise be to the God and Father of our Lord Jesus Christ, the Father of compassion and the God of all comfort, who comforts us in all our troubles, so that we can comfort those in any trouble with the comfort we ourselves have received from God." We experienced that. We started comforting those around us. We could comfort others because the Lord had comforted us. He spoke through us to the people. We were channels of living water, as the Lord had promised.

Next to the prison barracks where we were, there was a barracks full of Gypsies. We saw them frequently, and I remember that we prayed a lot for them. You can achieve so much through intercession. We did not meet many of them, but some time ago when a Gypsy lady in Germany was asked if she knew Jesus, she said, "Yes, I found Him when I was in a concentration camp. There Corrie ten Boom led me to Him. I know that Jesus died for me on the Cross. He died there for the whole world and for me too." You see, I had comforted her with the comfort God had given me.

In Luke 21:13 and 28, Jesus describes our times: "This will result in your being witnesses to them. . . . When these things begin to take place, stand up and lift up your heads, because your redemption is drawing near." You see, the Lord Jesus saw everything from God's perspective. He also sees everything that happens now from God's perspective.

God's plan is described in the Bible. What comfort Jesus gives in Revelation 21:5–6, ". . . I am making everything new," and "To him who is thirsty I will give to drink without cost from the spring of the water of life." What riches for you and me! Even if things get much worse, the best is still to come!

Let us pray. "Lord Jesus, come quickly and do what You promised and make all things new! Comfort us and give us the wonderful experience of passing on that comfort to others. Hallelujah. Amen."

Thirteen

God Gives Us Love

What does a Christian have if it is dark in the world? Love! In Africa a man came to a meeting with bandaged hands. I asked him how he had been injured. He said, "My neighbor's straw roof was on fire; I helped him to put it out and that's how my hands were burned."

Later I heard the whole story. The neighbor hated him and had set his roof on fire while his wife and children were asleep in the hut. They were in great danger. Fortunately, he was able to put out the fire in his house on time. But sparks flew over to the roof of the man who had set the house on fire and his house started to burn. There was no hate in the heart of this Christian; there was love for his enemy and he did everything he could to put out the fire in his neighbor's house. That is how his own hands were burned.

I already told how I experienced that love once myself, when I met a man who had been very cruel to my sister and me. He told me that he had found the Lord Jesus and confessed all his sins and now he was asking my forgiveness. There was bitterness in my heart when I thought of all he had done, but suddenly I thought of Romans 5:5: ". . . God has poured out his love into our hearts by the Holy Spirit." I said, "Thank You Lord that Your love is in my heart." Then I could say, "I forgive you for everything."

I was so happy, because Jesus has said that if we do not forgive, then we will not be forgiven. I couldn't do it, but Jesus in me could. On the cross Jesus said, "Father, forgive them for they do not know what they are doing." Jesus on the cross was the solution to our problem. What love, that God's Son carried our sins.

The love of God has been poured out in our hearts by the Holy Spirit, who has been given to us (Rom. 5:5). The love of God is great and strong; yes, we can speak of an ocean of love. That love gives us the strength to forgive and even to love our enemies. That love is a source of power and victory during the most terrible crises of our life, but also in everyday life.

We live in a danger zone. Hate, bitterness, fear, darkness, and self-centeredness are growing in the world around us, and we live in the midst of it. Television brings world events into our living rooms. The world is sick, and the danger of infection is serious. The demon of fear is so terribly strong. Hate and anger can quickly fill our hearts.

Fortunately, there is armor available (we can read about it in Ephesians 6), and we need that armor, right up to the last moment of our lives. It is Jesus Himself; we in Him and He in us (John 15:5). That is the new man, and the new man does not sin. Read about it in 1 John 2.

How can it be that such hate and fear can suddenly enter our hearts? That's the old man, who shows himself, and that's when the battle comes. But in Jesus we are conquerors (Rom. 8:37). The Holy Spirit produces fruit in us. Galatians 5:22 says, "The fruit of the Spirit is love, joy, peace, patience, kindness, goodness, faithfulness, gentleness and self-control."

The Lord Jesus used the example of the vine and the branches. A branch that remains in the vine produces fruit. If we remain in Jesus, He produces fruit through us. Then love regains the victory in our heart!

What we must and can do is confess our sins to Jesus. He forgives and cleanses us, and in a cleansed heart there is room for the fullness of God's Spirit. Hallelujah!

Let us pray. "Thank You, Lord, that You want to pour out Your love in our hearts through the Holy Spirit to each person who confesses his sin to You and is cleansed by Your blood. Savior, it is so dark in this world. There is so much hatred. Will You fill us with Your love so that we can pass it on to the poor people around us who are going through difficult times, when there is so much hate and fear? Keep us close to Your heart so that we, as branches of the vine, can produce the fruit of love. Thank You, Lord. Amen."

Fourteen

God Gives Us Security

What does a Christian have when it is dark in the world? Security!

In Colossians 3:3 we read, "hidden with Christ in God." It couldn't be safer! I sometimes show my hands as an example. I put my left hand over my thumb, and then I put my right hand over my left hand. You are the thumb. Jesus is the hand over your thumb; the right hand around it is God's—"hidden with Christ in God."

Some time ago I went to Japan. I went in obedience, but it was very difficult at first. I didn't know anyone, and in a country where you don't know the language, you have a strong sense of insecurity, especially if you are on your own. I opened my Bible and read 1 Peter 1:3–9, "Praise be to the God and Father of our Lord Jesus Christ! In his great mercy he has given us new birth into a living hope through the resurrection of Jesus Christ from the dead, and into an inheritance that can never perish, spoil, or fade—kept in heaven for you, who through faith are shielded by God's power until the coming of the salvation that is ready to be revealed in the last time. In this you greatly rejoice, though now for a little while you may have had to suffer grief in all kinds of trials. These have come so that your faith—of greater worth than gold, which perishes even though refined by fire—may be proved genuine and may result in praise, glory, and honor when Jesus Christ is revealed. Though you have not seen him, you love him; and even though you do not see him now, you believe in him and are filled with an inexpressible and glorious joy, for you are receiving the goal of your faith, the salvation of your souls."

What security! We are being kept for an inheritance; the inheritance is being kept for us. I saw this promise briefly from God's perspective. Things soon went really well in Japan. It was wonderful how the Lord opened hearts and doors for an exceptionally blessed ten months.

Obedience is extremely important. Love and obedience belong together. Even when it storms, there can still be peace. Jesus was obedient; He was prepared to die on a cross for you and me. What love!

In the center of a hurricane everything is quiet. I once experienced a hurricane in America. The storm passed just above us. It seemed as if we were in the middle of the storm; all about us was a raging wind. Heavy trees hit the ground and suddenly everything was quiet; nothing moved. The man sitting next to me said, "We are in the middle of the hurricane. It's quiet." It was only a brief moment; then the next half of the hurricane came. The real peace came when the storm had passed completely.

If we are hidden with Jesus in God, then peace remains. We are not afraid, even if the earth gives way and the mountains fall into the heart of the sea (Ps. 46:2). Even if it is night, we can experience the promise that "He who dwells in the shelter of the Most High will rest in the shadow of the Almighty" (Ps. 91:1). Hallelujah, what a sure security!

Shall we pray? "Thank You, Lord Jesus, that You give us certainty in the midst of uncertainty. Thank You that we are hidden with You in God. Listen, Lord, to those who now surrender to You. How marvelous that he, that she, is safe in Your arms. Amen."

Fifteen

How Can I Know What God Wants of Me?

3/8/00

We read in Isaiah 30:21, "Whether you turn to the right or to the left, your ears will hear a voice behind you, saying, 'This is the way; walk in it.'" Is that really true? Does God really lead His children?

Today I want to talk to you about what the Holy Spirit has to say to us about guidance, because that is often a problem for many people—sometimes for me too. There are many who say, "I never hear anything when I ask for guidance." But then I ask myself, Are you listening? Sometimes we have to wait on the Lord. But waiting in itself can be a blessing, if we do it in the presence of the Lord. That's what our "quiet time" is so good for.

If you are spiritually confused and you want to hear God's voice clearly, remain in His presence until the confusion changes. Much can happen during a time of waiting on the Lord. He sometimes changes pride to humility and doubt to faith and peace; yes, and even sometimes desire into purity. The Lord can and will do that. We must understand that sometimes the Lord's silence is His way of teaching us to grow, just as a mother calmly allows her child to fall and stand up again. If God sometimes allows conflicts, it may be His way of training us.

Some people say, "Oh, but it's very selfish to ask God for guidance." Do you know who whispers that to them? It is the enemy. The devil is terribly afraid of children of God who safely walk in the Lord's hand. It is God's will to guide us. Let's look at what the Bible says about His guidance: "I will instruct you and teach you in the way you should go; I will counsel you and watch over you" (Ps. 32:8). Could it be any clearer? And in Psalm 48:14, "For this God is our God for ever and ever; he will be our guide even to the end." Yes, it is God's will to lead us.

How come we so often do not hear the voice of the Lord? I believe it is because our sins are a barrier between Him and us. As the Psalmist says, his sins prevented him from looking up. Satan's work is sometimes like a mist on the outside of the window of our souls that hides the light of God. Our sinful desire is like the dirt on the inside of the window. Occasionally God puts His hand on the window; then He is very close by. If you don't receive guidance or hear the voice of God, the reason is often disobedience.

When I left a concentration camp during the war, I said (I will never forget this), "Now I want to travel over the whole world. I'll go wherever God leads, but one thing: I hope He never sends me to Germany." From my experiences in prisons I had a wrong, false picture of Germany. That was no surprise. I was therefore only partially obedient—anywhere Lord, but not Germany. I went to America, and I asked for guidance, but I didn't receive an answer. That was terrible! I asked the Lord, "Lord, is there maybe some sin between You and me?" I received a very clear answer: "Germany." I repented before the Lord and said, "Lord, then I'll go to Germany too."

I went to Germany, and I actually found that nowhere in the world were there as many open doors as in Germany. My best friends live there, but I also found my enemies there. I learned that if you love your enemies, you touch the ocean of God's love as never before. I'd learned my lesson: obedience! Not "Yes, but . . . ," but "Yes, Father." Peter said, "No, my Lord." But you can't say "no" if you say "My Lord," and you can't say "My Lord" if you say "no." It is most important to be obedient, because disobedience can make everything very dark.

God leads in three ways. First in our prayers, then through His Word (the Bible), and then through circumstances. It is so wonderful that in prayer, we don't only have the privilege of speaking to God, but of listening to Him, as well. That doesn't happen immediately; you have to get used to it. As Job says, "Submit to God and be at peace with him" (Job 22:21). In hidden companionship with God, we learn to hear His voice.

It is the devil who holds us back so that we cannot hear God's voice—that is his purpose. There are two rivals for God's voice, namely, yourself and the devil. We have to learn to differentiate between these voices.

God's commandments—His words—are simple, pure, and true, but those of the devil are complicated. He uses doubt, rebellion, and lies. Compare the following two voices. In Genesis 2:16–17 God says, "You are free to eat from any tree in the garden; but you must not eat from the tree of the knowledge of good and evil. . . ." Then we read what Satan says in Genesis 3:1: "Did God really say, 'You must not eat from any tree in the garden'?" You see, Satan twists God's words; and see how Satan loves to argue. Eve fell for it and began to argue too. Another difference is that Satan is always in a hurry, but God has time because He has eternity. His commands can often come very suddenly, but He always allows time to work them out.

It is not hard for the Lord to lead, and, therefore, asking God for guidance gives you a wonderful opportunity for hidden companionship with Him. It is such a comfort to know that before we were born, God had already made His plan for us. He gave us gifts and qualities, and He will surely not waste them now that you are a Christian! He, our good Shepherd, knows your physical, emotional, and spiritual needs better than you do. He said, "I will never leave you nor forsake you" (Josh. 1:5). He knows the end from the beginning and can allow all that you do and experience work for the good of yourself and others, if only we could better understand what it means to be a child of God.

When you accept God as your Savior, He, your Redeemer and Lord, makes you a child of God. If you have not done that yet, I hope that you accept Him now. But we have to understand what it means to be a child of God. God is our Father, who loves us. We are a part of Him. It is not hard work for Him to lead us; He thinks it's wonderful, and there is nothing too great for His omnipotence and nothing too small for His love.

Prayer: "Oh Father, we thank You that we are Your children and that You are a good Shepherd. Teach us through Your Spirit to hear Your voice clearly. Thank You. Hallelujah. Amen."

Sixteen

God's Guidance

oday I want to speak again about guidance and answer
this question: May you ask God for a sign? Yes, I think
so! Gideon asked for a sign, and he received it. Often God con-
firms what He has already said to His obedient child through
a sign. You must be sure, however, that you ask with the right
motive—not, for example, with the intention of seeking a
shortcut to getting your own way or ending your quiet time
more quickly. Playing heads and tails is much quicker than
praying and listening to God's voice.

When I worked in Germany shortly after the war, I lived in
one building with about four hundred people, all refugees. It
was terrible. I never felt the needs of postwar Germany so much
as when I lived there with these people. After a while I was
exhausted. In that period I received an invitation from America
to speak at a student's club, InterVarsity Christian Fellowship,
and I really wanted to go. But then I grew a little hesitant
because if you really want something, it could be that you say
rather superficially, "Well, that must be God's guidance to go."

I asked for a sign. I said, "Lord, if I get a free trip to America, that will be a sign for me that I may go to America. I will

also buy chairs for the refugees if you give me the money for it."
During that time I had about one hundred and sixty refugees
to take care of, and I had no money to buy chairs for them. My
friends said, "That means you won't be going to America." I
said, "Why not? God can perform a miracle. Surely He can give
me a free trip?"

I went to the Oostzee company in Amsterdam. I can still see
myself standing there amongst the sailors to sign on as a stewardess. The captain at the quay looked at me strangely when I
said what I had come for. He looked me up and down from
head to toe, and I am sure he thought, Now, that's a rather old
stewardess. He said, "Do you know that if you sign on as a stewardess on one of our cargo ships, you have to sign on for the
return journey on the same ship and you can stay in America for
ten days?" I said, "No, ten months." "Exactly," he said, "that's
what I thought. You're not coming for a job. You want to get to
America a bit cheaply." "Yes, that's right," I replied. He then
said, "That's out of the question!"

I think he saw that I was a bit disappointed. Then he asked,
"What's your name?" "Corrie ten Boom," I replied. He said, "Did
you write *A Prisoner, and Yet . . .*?" We had a nice conversation
about loving your enemies because he thought it very odd that
I had returned to Germany. He said, "I won't be the one who
prevents you from getting a free trip!" I got my trip and went to
America. As soon as I arrived in America, I received a donation,
and I used it to buy chairs for my refugees.

Yes, I do believe that we may ask for a sign, and it is often
like that, too, if you seek God's guidance. As a Good Shepherd,
He knows what His sheep need. He loves His sheep. He loves
you, more than the best earthly shepherd loves his sheep.

I had asked the Lord what my schedule should be for the coming year. The Lord told me very clearly that I should go to Vietnam. Now, I didn't like that at all; I found it quite difficult, but I waited. Then I went to a conference for evangelists in Berlin. There, Bob Pearce of World Vision approached me— the man who is always at the place of catastrophes and great need. He is an enormous blessing! When he saw me, the first thing he asked was, "Corrie, when are you going to come with me to Vietnam?" I said, "As soon as you ask me, I'll come." The same thing happened again, when I was working in Germany for the American Army. God blessed my time there, and I was enjoying it immensely. Then the Army chaplain said, "Why don't you go to Vietnam? There are 300,000 American soldiers there." I knew what to do.

You see, that's what it means to have the Lord guide us very clearly. He not only wants to lead us, but if we listen obediently and follow Him, then we are at peace. If you have an important decision to make, or even a small one, it is good to make your decision with the guidance of the Lord.

First, we have to check whether we are obedient to God's will; then we have to question our motives for wanting to go there or to do that. We can test our motives with the Bible. The Sermon on the Mount (Matt. 5–7) is a wonderful norm by which we can test our motives, as is 1 Corinthians 13, or whatever Scripture the Lord leads us to. Always make sure your decision is made in God's presence, when you are really together with Him. This will help you to better distinguish His voice and be certain of His blessing on your decision. It is a wonderful experience to discuss your plans with the Lord. You develop such a warm relationship with Him. He is a very, very Good

Shepherd. He loves us, and He delights in leading us. We have to realize that He loves to guide us.

I also wanted to talk about human advice. Yes, God also speaks through human advice, but we must be careful because often this can lead to confusion. Imagine if Samuel had asked people their opinions on who would make a suitable king of Israel. Do you think one person would have said, "Hey, the boy walking behind the sheep, you should choose him to be king?"

Human advice, by itself, can bring confusion. Often the best advice is offered by people who don't know themselves that they are being used by God. A church service, especially a prayer meeting, can be helpful—praying together with others and waiting together on God, first in silence and then praying aloud. The Lord Jesus wants to be our guide, when there is darkness around us, to light our path.

"Thank You, Lord Jesus, that You came and thank You that You are a friend who never deserts us. Lord, teach us by Your Spirit to better distinguish Your voice. Thank You that You want to do this. Thank You for Your great love. Thank You that You carried the sins of the whole world on the cross, and our sins in particular. Thank You that You have given us the answer to two great problems in our lives: the problem of sin and the problem of death. How You loved us; how You still love us. Thank You, Lord Jesus. Amen."

Seventeen

Going Where God Sends You

One morning I spoke in a church in Copenhagen, Denmark. The text was Romans 12:1 "I urge you, brothers, in view of God's mercy, to offer your bodies as living sacrifices, holy and pleasing to God—this is your spiritual act of worship." I told my audience that they had to give their bodies as a pleasing sacrifice to the Lord. I said that although I was an elderly woman, I still wanted to give myself completely to Jesus and do what He desired me to do and go where he desired me to go—to be obedient even to the point of death.

After the service, two nurses approached me. They invited me for a cup of coffee in their apartment. I was very tired. A cup of coffee seemed very appealing, and I gratefully accepted their invitation. But I was not prepared for the steep climb to their room. Many of the houses in Copenhagen are very old and have no elevators, and the nurses lived on the tenth floor.... "Oh Lord, I don't think I can make it," I said. But the nurses were so insistent that I should visit them that I didn't dare refuse. When I at last reached the fifth floor my old heart was beating heavily and my legs refused to go a step further. I saw a chair and sat down. I said to the nurses, "Go on to your room. When I've rested I'll come too."

I asked the Lord, "Why do I have to walk up so many flights of stairs after such a busy day, Lord?" The answer came immediately: "Because there will be such a great blessing up there. It will even give joy to the angels of God." I looked at the winding stairs, which I could see going on right to the top. "Maybe I am going to heaven," I thought, "that will give joy to the angels." I counted the steps. There were a hundred or more. But if God said that the work would make the angels rejoice, I had to go. I stood up and started to climb again. At last I reached the tenth floor, and when I arrived in the nurses' room, I found a table brightly laid. The meal had been prepared by the parents of one of the nurses. I knew that I only had a little time, and I knew too that in one way or another, God was going to give a blessing. So I soon started a conversation.

"Tell me," I asked the nurse's mother, "was it long ago that you got to know the Lord Jesus?" "I have never met Him," she said, a little surprised at my question. I said, "Don't you want to come to Him? He loves you. I have talked of Him in more than sixty countries, and I have never met anyone who regretted giving his heart to Jesus, and neither will you if you do."

I opened the Bible and read her texts that made salvation through the Lord Jesus very clear. She listened with great interest. Then I asked, "Shall we speak together with the Lord?" I prayed and both the nurses prayed with me. At last, the mother put her hands together and said, "Lord Jesus, I actually know a great deal about You. I just read the Bible, but I now pray for You to come into my heart. I need salvation and cleansing. I know that You died on the cross for the sins of the whole world and for my sin too. Please Lord Jesus, come into my heart and make me a child of God. Amen."

I looked up and saw tears of joy on the faces of the young nurses. They had prayed so much for the parents, and now their prayers had been answered. I turned to the father, who had quietly listened to everything. "What do you think of this?" I asked. "I have never made a decision for the Lord Jesus," he said seriously, "but I have listened to everything you said to my wife and I now know the way. I will pray to Jesus too, for Him to save me." He bowed his head, and from his lips came a joyful, serious prayer as he gave his life to Jesus Christ. I know that there were angels around us who were praising God. It says in the Bible that the angels rejoice over every sinner who repents.

"Thank You, Lord," I whispered, as I went down the many stairs, "that You let me walk up all these steps to the top. The next time, Lord, help Corrie ten Boom listen to her own sermons, so that I am ready to go where You lead, even if it is steps up to the tenth floor."

Let us pray together. "Lord, we thank You that You give us the willingness to go where You lead us, and we thank You that we stand on victory ground if we strive and work in obedience to You. We thank You that You in no way drive away those who come to You, but that You feel great joy when we place our lives in Your hands. Thank You for the people there in Denmark. Will You bless them, Lord; and will You bless us and make us a blessing. Hallelujah! Amen."

Eighteen

Have You Left Your First Love?

I recall an experience in Africa. It was during a sort of one-year holiday—a Sabbath year we called it. I had enjoyed living in a house where missionaries and others could rest. The house had a beautiful tropical garden overlooking Lake Victoria. The climate was tropical, but because of the altitude, it was not too warm. I very much enjoyed the rest, especially since I was able to sleep in the same bed every night. During the previous twenty years, I had slept in more than one thousand different beds.

I could work, fortunately—meetings in churches and universities, clubs and prisons—but not more than three or four times a week. Now the year of rest prescribed by the doctor was over. On November 1, I was free to leave. My assistant Connie and I laid all the invitations and a map of the world on the bed and asked God to guide us as to how we should prepare the coming program. We had grown accustomed to not making plans first and then asking God for His signature. No, we waited for guidance from the Lord first, and then we endorsed His plans.

It was a nice schedule. Four months more in Africa, two months in Eastern Europe, three months in America . . . but I didn't feel happy. Was it really necessary to travel again? I discussed it with the Lord. That's always good, if your heart is not completely happy with His guidance. "I want what You want, Lord. I want to work wherever You lead me, but there are plenty of opportunities here, in churches, clubs, and prisons." I felt so happy. Of course it was good in God's eyes—I wouldn't have to travel, and I could sleep in the same bed every night.

"You have a visitor," Connie called, "a brother from Rwanda." A black minister came up to me. "We are so happy that you are coming to Rwanda," he said. "Five years ago you visited us. You said then how the Lord Jesus had never let you down. Your stories were so good, but it didn't mean much to us. We had never been in prison. But a couple of years ago there was a war. Many, including me, went to jail and your stories of your experiences helped so much. That's why we are so happy you are coming back."

That was just what I didn't want! To change the subject somewhat, I asked some questions. "What kind of church do you have? What message do you think your people need?" Without a moment's hesitation the minister opened his Bible and read from Revelation 2: "To the angel of the church in Ephesus write: These are the words of him who holds the seven stars in his right hand and walks among the seven golden lampstands: I know your deeds, your hard work and your perseverance. I know that you cannot tolerate wicked men, that you have tested those who claim to be apostles but are not, and have found them false. You have persevered and have endured hardships for my name, and have not grown weary. Yet I hold this against you: You have forsaken your first love. Remember the height from which you have fallen! Repent and do the things you did at first. If you do not repent, I will come to you and remove your lampstand from its place." That was the message for Ephesus and for Rwanda. For Corrie ten Boom, too, was my echo!

How I had changed! Twenty years before, I had gotten out of jail, weak and ill, but I was interested in two important things. First, the salvation of souls. I could tell them about Jesus, about how He had accomplished on the cross everything that was necessary to redeem them from sin. I could tell them about the wonderful glory of being a child of God and invite them to come to Him. Secondly, I was interested in glorifying the Name of the Lord by talking about the special miracles I had experienced, about who the Lord Jesus was to me when I was in prison, and about how He had never let me down. Yes, that was twenty years ago; that's what I was interested in then. And now? I was interested in my bed!

I had forsaken my first love. I opened my Bible and read, "If you do not repent. . . ." (Rev. 2:5). There was such great joy in my heart. The door to repentance was wide open. I asked for forgiveness. The Lord forgave me and cleansed me with His blood. Hallelujah! I obeyed God's program, and what a blessing it was. Had I returned to my first love? No, much better than that. The Lord forgave me and cleansed my heart with His blood; He fills a cleansed heart with His Holy Spirit and His love (Rom. 5:5). His love, the fruit of the Spirit, is far more than my first love ever was. Have you forsaken your first love? I have a wonderful message for you. The door of repentance is wide open.

"Thank You, Lord Jesus, for the ocean of love that we can possess when You cleanse our hearts and fill them with Your Holy Spirit. Listen, Lord, to whoever now says, 'Savior, I have forsaken my first love. Forgive me, cleanse my heart, fill me with Your Spirit and Your love.' Thank You, Lord Jesus. Amen."

Nineteen

God Works Through Our Helplessness

I once read in a newsletter that if we say that the Lord may use us, then we should not be surprised if we sometimes face impossible situations in life.

If we have given ourselves completely to the Lord, then He will show His greatness through our helplessness. We read in Luke 9 about the feeding of the five thousand. In verse 13 the Lord Jesus said to His disciples, "You give them something to eat," and verse 17 says, "They all ate and were satisfied, and the disciples picked up twelve basketfuls of broken pieces that were left over."

I was once in a country where there was much hatred. Divorce was prevalent; the streets were extremely dangerous, especially in the evenings. Murders were common. I heard about an old lady who was murdered for $10. I had a message for that country. I had experienced myself that if the Lord Jesus tells us to love our enemies, He gives us the love He asks of us (Rom. 5:5). I wanted to tell them, "Friends, you don't need to try yourself, you can't; but if you open your heart to the Lord

Jesus, then He will bring God's love into your heart through the Holy Spirit."

When the Lord clearly told me to visit that country, I encountered much opposition. "Stay in Holland," people said, "we don't need you here." I told them, "The Lord has guided me to come to this country." "Rubbish," answered the people, "that doesn't happen—guidance from the Lord, that's fanaticism."

Fortunately I was not discouraged. A little while ago, I went there again. I was asked to speak on television. One thing led to another and I spoke eight times in front of the big lamps that shone in my face, opposite cameras that broadcast my words and face to millions of people. Yes! I was able to tell four million people that the Holy Spirit brought love for my enemies into my heart.

I had hated the people who had put me, my family, and my friends in prison during World War II. Those people had on their consciences the death of my father, who, at the age of eighty-four, had died ten days after entering prison, and the death of my sister Betsie, who died after ten months of terrible suffering. But because the Holy Spirit had given me the love of God in my heart, I was able to forgive and love those same people I had hated!

I was eighty-one years old and could not travel very much, but God performed a miracle. Millions of people were able to hear my message. A mother wrote to me, "Now I can forgive the murderer of my eighteen-year-old daughter." She was one of the many people God reached by letting me speak on television. Feeding five thousand people with five loaves and two fishes—impossible! But Jesus said, "You give them something to eat," and the disciples obeyed, and a miracle took place: twelve baskets filled with pieces of food were left.

Do you have an impossible job to do? Has the Lord told you to do it? Go ahead! When we pray, we enter God's domain from the domain of our inability. He is conqueror and makes us more than conquerors. It is not bad if we feel weak, if our inability is a reality to us. That's exactly when the Lord does miracles. Paul said, "When I am weak, then I am strong." Do you know why I thought it so important that these people in that country learned to forgive? Jesus said that if we do not forgive, we will not be forgiven, and we break down the bridge that we need for ourselves. Jesus is coming again very soon, and we must be prepared—by being in good relationship with God and with others. We can't get it together ourselves, however hard we try. But if we place our weak hand in the strong hand of Jesus, then He does it. Jesus is looking forward to His return to earth and it is He who is preparing us for His return. Surrender to Him completely. He who began a good work in you will bring it to completion on that day—the day of His second coming.

Our family had a little savings box, and when it was full, it was given to missions. "A dime in the blessing box!" was my Mother's cry when kind, unexpected guests arrived. If we sold an expensive watch from our watchmakers' shop, if the Lord saved us from an accident just in the nick of time, or if we arrived home safely after a journey or camp, the blessing box was put on the table. Try it sometime! It accentuates our blessings wonderfully! You become doubly thankful for them. "Count your blessings, name them one by one, and it will surprise you what the Lord has done!"

Keep looking in the right direction in everything you do—that is so important. I often say, "Keep looking up and kneeling down." One day I met a missionary who was desperate because Christians were continually being killed near her home. "Look down on the storms and terrible events around us, down from on high," I said, "from the heavenly realms where Jesus' victory is the greatest reality." This is only possible through the Holy Spirit.

I remember from my time in prison in Ravensbrück, where so many men and women were killed, that Betsie and I sometimes walked in the prison grounds before we were called for registration in the mornings at 4:30 A.M. Then God performed a miracle. We experienced His presence so vividly that it was as if we were talking to one another. Betsie would say something, then I would say something, and then the Lord would say something—and both Betsie and I heard what He said. I cannot explain it, but it was wonderful. We saw then that even though everything was terrible, we could rely on the fact that God did not have any problems, only plans. There is never panic in heaven! You can only hold on to that reality through faith because it seemed then, and often seems now, as if the devil is the victor. But God is faithful, and His plans never fail! He knows the future. He knows the way.

Watchman Nee once said that surrender to the Lord means turning around one hundred and eighty degrees—that means a renewed person and renewed vision. Even John, the disciple whom Jesus loved, had to have his eyes on his eternal Lord (Rev. 1). We are not ready for the battle until we have seen the Lord, for Jesus is the answer to all problems.

Look to the Lord and you will gain His perspective on the difficulties. Second Corinthians 4:17–18 says, "For our light and momentary troubles are achieving for us an eternal glory that far outweighs them all. So we fix our eyes not on what is seen, but on what is unseen. For what is seen is temporary, but what is unseen is eternal." You don't understand? That doesn't matter. Just believe. Psalm 10:14 says, "But you, O God, do see trouble and grief; you consider it to take it in hand."

"Lord, keep us close to Your heart, so that we see everything in and around us from Your perspective. Then we will not fear because we know that You never make a mistake. Hallelujah. Amen."

Twenty

Reasons for Demon Possession

*H*ow is it that people become possessed by evil spirits or come under their influence? We can often find the reasons in occult sin. That is very clear and apparent with fortune-telling. In Deuteronomy 18:10–12 we read, "Let no one be found among you who sacrifices his son or daughter in the fire, who practices divination or sorcery, interprets omens, engages in witchcraft, or casts spells, or who is a medium or spiritist or who consults the dead. Anyone who does these things is detestable to the LORD, and because of these detestable practices the LORD your God will drive out those nations before you."

When I was working in Germany after the war, people often talked to me about not being able to pray. They could not concentrate when they read the Bible or listened to a sermon. They were often plagued by thoughts of suicide—a very clear indication that a demonic influence is present. I later discovered the reason. Just after the war, many men and boys in Germany were still missing. People didn't know if they were in a concentration camp in Russia or if they had died in battle. This uncertainty was awful, so people went to see fortune-tellers. Whether they got any correct information, I do not know, but this was the reason for the darkness that I later saw during my pastoral work there. The door had been opened to dark powers due to this sin. Usually it was not difficult to convince people that this is a sin in the eyes of the Lord. The Bible is very clear about this in Deuteronomy 18: it is an abomination in God's eyes because it is apparent that someone is asking for help from the enemy instead of trusting in God's power.

It was marvelous to explain to them how they could be set free (1 John 1:7, 9). I told them that if they knew that they had sinned, they could bring this sin to the Lord, confess it, and ask for forgiveness. I saw this promise become reality. The Lord forgave them and cleansed them with His blood and filled them with His Holy Spirit. The fruit of the Spirit is, among other things, peace and joy (Gal. 5:22)!

Taking part in spiritist experiments can also open the door to occult darkness. Very frequently, when I warn against fortune-telling and spiritism, I ask if people have taken part in it, and the answer I often get is, "I only did it for a joke," or "I didn't believe in it."

When I get this reply, I use this example. A while ago in Germany, before the wall had been built, half of the city was forbidden to West Berliners. Part of the border passed through a forest. If a West Berliner was caught playing in the forest on East German territory, he would be arrested. It would not help if he said, "I was only playing, or I did it for a joke." If you are on enemy territory, then you are in the enemy's power. The same applies when you jokingly commit occult sins.

Another very dangerous sin is to wear amulets. You cannot be too careful about this. I heard of a girl who was always sick.

Someone gave her an amulet to wear around her neck. The illness was immediately cured, but the child became very depressed. She never laughed. When she was twelve, she tried to commit suicide. An evangelist visited her and asked if she had an amulet. She gave it to him, but she begged him not to open it! Nevertheless, he opened it and found a piece of paper, on which was written, "I command you, Satan, to keep this body healthy until you have its soul in hell." They destroyed the amulet, and the child was freed, but immediately she became seriously ill. She was later cured by the laying on of hands in the name of Jesus.

Apart from fortune-telling and wearing charms and amulets, contact with false teachers or with people who exercise demonic influence (for example, palm readers, astrologers, or magnetic healers) can be a reason for darkness, as can reading horoscopes or occult books, experimenting with hypnotism, attempting to contact the dead, or carelessly associating with the sins of others or with demonized people. For good reason, Paul warns Timothy against hasty laying on of hands.

In Indonesia, where there was a great revival, it was common to see people surrender to the Lord, repent of their sins, and burn and destroy all idols, amulets, and occult books. As we live in such dangerous times, all compromise is an especially great threat. If we choose Jesus' side, we stand as children of light in the midst of a dark generation. But our choice must be very definite. What joy that there is forgiveness and salvation in Jesus.

Let us pray: "Dear Father, in Jesus' name we pray that You will allow us to clearly see if there is any compromise with Satan or his demons in our lives and hearts. Thank You that You want to free us and strengthen us, that You want to cleanse us with the blood of Jesus, Your dear Son, and strengthen us through Your Holy Spirit. Hallelujah! Amen."

Twenty-One

The Courage of Faith

A few years ago, I was in a country far from here, and I had to speak on a Sunday morning in church. When I looked at the people, I could see fear written all over their faces. You could feel the tension. No wonder. Every day during the previous week, a large number of Christians had received a piece of paper telling them to report to the police. At night they heard shooting in the beautiful sports stadium just outside the town. All those who reported were shot. That happened every day; each time more Christians.

I didn't understand the political background at all, but I did know that there was a new government. As I was sitting in the church, I saw people looking at each other anxiously. I could easily understand what they were thinking: Will he be killed this week? Will she still be alive next week? Will I still be here?

I asked the Lord for a word from the Bible to give to these people. The Lord gave me 1 Peter 4:12–14: "Dear friends, do not be surprised at the painful trial you are suffering, as though something strange were happening to you. But rejoice that you participate in the sufferings of Christ, so that you may be overjoyed when his glory is revealed. If you are insulted because of the name of Christ, you are blessed, for the Spirit of glory and of God rests on you."

"If you have to suffer and maybe die for Jesus soon," I said to the people, "then He will ensure that you have all the courage and grace that you need in time. Don't be afraid. Don't forget that there is a crown in heaven for all martyrs. The Spirit of God, the Spirit of glory, will rest on you, says Peter."

There was great joy in the church. When the service was over, someone began to sing, "In the sweet by and by, we shall meet at the beautiful shore. . . ." The people kept singing that song as they left the church, and I heard that song for quite some time as they walked down the road. I soon found out that roughly half of those people in the church were killed that week.

At midnight, we could hear shooting continually. We worked in a kind of radio studio there. One morning we had a meeting in the building. It was well insulated against sound from outside. When we left the building after the meeting, there were groups of people on the street. "What happened?" we asked. "Didn't you hear? There was a storm, and lightning hit the stadium, right where the gunpowder and weapons were kept. The whole building was blown up. That was God's judgment for killing the Christians."

Some time ago I was at a large international evangelists' congress in Lausanne. I met people from many countries, including a missionary from the country where these events had taken place. I asked, "How are things going with your radio station?" "Oh, wonderful. The studio was closed for a year, and now we have permission to broadcast again. Day and night the gospel is heard on all sides." "That's wonderful," I replied, "and tell me, how are the friends I worked with?" She waited for a minute. Then she said, "They were all killed." She saw how shocked I was. She put her hand on my shoulder and said, with a smile on her face, "They were promoted ahead of us."

Yes, the Spirit of glory rested on them. I saw it from God's side. If you are close to the Lord, then you can see things from His side—a bird's-eye view from heaven. Then you can smile, even when you speak of terrible things that have happened.

That is what you and I need—to see things from God's perspective. Then we know that He does not make mistakes, and that our present suffering is worth nothing compared to the glory that is to come. God works out His plan on earth. Even if we go through great trials and the trials are, perhaps, even deeper than we experience now, we can know that the best is yet to come! That is a great comfort.

"Thank You, Lord, that You always give Your courage and strength in time, even if we have to suffer and perhaps die for You. Allow us through Your Holy Spirit to always see things from Your perspective, because then we need not fear, even if the earth gives way and the mountains fall into the sea. Thank You, Lord! Amen."

Twenty-Two

Are You Afraid of Death?

There is a story of two monks who said to one another, "Whoever dies first has to come back and tell the other what heaven is like." One died and came back to the other the next day and said two words, "Totaliter aliter," that is, "totally different." The Bible says that too: "No eye has seen, no ear has heard, no mind has conceived what God has prepared for those who love him" (1 Cor. 2:9).

The Bible says that man is destined to die once and, after that, to face judgment. So if we know it's coming, we ought to prepare for it. I am not frightened of death. "How can you be so sure?" you might ask. My reply is that I know death. I've looked into its eyes, not occasionally, but steadily for a few months when I was in a barracks in a concentration camp that looked out onto a crematorium. Every day about six hundred bodies were burned—the bodies of prisoners who died or were killed. When I saw the smoke from the chimney of the crematorium, I asked myself, "When will it be time for you to be killed?" I didn't know then that a few weeks before prisoners of my age were to be killed, I would be released miraculously. I noticed then that I was not afraid. Perhaps you are thinking,

"What courage!" But it wasn't courage. It was the Lord Jesus who gave me security. The Bible says, "Where, O death, is your victory? Where, O death, is your sting?" (1 Cor. 15:55). I thank God for the victory of the Lord Jesus Christ. I know that about two thousand years ago the Lord Jesus bore my sins, and then He said, "It is finished." The answer is on the cross. The Bible sums it up so clearly: "If we confess our sins, He is faithful and just and will forgive us our sins and purify us from all unrighteousness" (1 John 1:9). Believe in the Lord Jesus and you will be blessed.

Many years ago, I talked at a girls' club about God's judgment—that Jesus is the Judge who judges us. Romans 8:34 was my text: ". . . Christ Jesus, who died—more than that, who was raised to life—is at the right hand of God and is also interceding for us."

Pietje Stevens, a particularly sweet girl, looked worried. Suddenly her face lit up. "Oh how wonderful," she said, "our judge is also our advocate." Jesus Christ, the Judge, at the right hand of God, is also the one who pleads for us. What a relief. It wasn't long after that I visited Pietje in the hospital. I'll never forget it. She was dying. "Pietje, do you know that our judge is also our advocate?" She whispered, "Thank You, Jesus."

The Bible says that the wages of sin is death. The grace that God gives is eternal life in the Lord Jesus Christ. When Pietje Stevens died, I looked at her and knew that she was safe with the Lord, who does not make mistakes.

Is everything okay with you? Do you know the Lord Jesus? Have you asked Him to live in your heart? Have you asked for forgiveness of your sins and said, "Thank You, Jesus, that You died at the cross for me? Thank You that I am forgiven?" Then you, too, can say, "Thank You that You will be the judge and also my advocate." Jesus says, "Come to Me, all of you," and that includes you.

"Oh, Lord Jesus, we thank You that You have such great love and that we may all come to You. Thank You for what You did on the cross, and what You will do as judge and advocate. Hallelujah! What a Savior. Amen."

Twenty-Three

What Is Your Final Destination?

I was once on a mission plane. That is always such a wonderful experience! In a large plane you forget that you are up high in the air but in a small plane you see the ground beneath you, the sky around you, and you feel really dependent on the Lord's protection. I asked the pilot, "Where are we going?" He answered immediately because he was in no doubt as to our destination.

I remember that I once had to order a plane ticket in the country formerly known as Formosa. It was a long itinerary: Formosa—Sydney (Australia)—Auckland—Sydney—Cape Town (South Africa)—Tel Aviv (Israel)—Amsterdam. The young lady in the office asked me, "What is your final destination?" "Heaven," I replied. "How do you spell that?" she asked. "H-e-a-v-e-n," I said. She wrote it under the word Amsterdam, but then she suddenly understood what I meant. "I don't mean that," she said. I remarked, "Oh no? But I do mean it, but you don't need to write it down, I already have my ticket." "What do you mean by that?" she asked. I explained, "About two thousand years ago, someone ordered my ticket to heaven. I just needed to accept it from Him. That was the Lord Jesus, when He bore the punishment for my sins on the cross."

A man from Formosa who was standing in front of us, turned around and said, "That's true." I asked him, "It's good you know that; do you have a reservation in heaven?" "I certainly do," he said. "I accepted Jesus as my Savior and He made me a child of God. Every child of God has a place reserved in the Father's house with its many mansions, where Jesus has prepared a place for all those who know Him as their Redeemer."

"Brother, come here," I said. "Miss, if you don't have a reserved seat in a plane, you can get into great difficulty; I've experienced that. But if you don't have a place reserved in heaven, you are in far deeper trouble. Brother, you must make sure your colleague isn't too late to make a reservation." Was that a joke? No, I was serious, and I'm serious when I ask you, "Are you sure you'll get to heaven when you die?"

If you are not sure, then I can give you a wonderful message. Come to Jesus. He said, "Come to me, all you who are weary and burdened, and I will give you rest" (Matt. 11:28). If the Son sets you free, you will be free indeed. To those who accept Him, He gives the right to become a child of God. Pray this prayer: "Lord Jesus, I am a sinner. I need redemption and forgiveness. I believe that You died on the cross for my sins. Will You forgive me and give me a clean heart and make me a child of God?"

I was so happy when I received my ticket a few days later. My finances are always in the realm of God's miracles. He is my heavenly Treasurer. When I need money—and I often do—I say to Him, "Father in heaven, in the Bible it says that You have cattle on a thousand hills. That's quite a lot. Will You sell Your cows and give me the money?" He always does so. I never need to ask people for money; I trust the Lord to tell them. This time, too, the money for the ticket arrived just on time. I leafed through my book of tickets with great thankfulness in my heart: "Formosa—Sydney—Auckland—Sydney—Tel Aviv—Cape Town—Amsterdam" . . . but that was different from what I had ordered!

I picked up the phone and said, "Miss, you've made a mistake. I ordered: Sydney, Cape Town and then Tel Aviv in Israel. And you've twisted that around. I don't make my travel plans myself; I ask God what His will is, and I want to obey Him."

"But the way you ordered your trip is impossible to arrange. There is no direct connection between Australia and South Africa. There are no islands in the Indian Ocean where a stopover can be made, so you first have to go to Tel Aviv and then Cape Town in South Africa." "So, that's the problem," I said, "Maybe we have to pray to God for an island in the Indian Ocean."

Half an hour later she phoned me. "Miss, did you pray for an island in the Indian Ocean? We just received a telegram from Quantas that they have leased Cocos Island, and you can now fly direct from Australia via Cocos Island to South Africa."

What wonderful music there is in following and obeying the Lord! God often specializes in the impossible. Hallelujah!

Let us pray: "Thank You, Lord, that we can tell You about our problems and ask You about everything. Thank You that You Yourself make us want to obey You. Lord, I thank You that You are listening to her and to him, who at this moment is saying, 'Lord Jesus, I want to be sure that I will go to heaven. I understand that You are calling me today to come to You. Lord, I come to You now and pray that You will forgive my sins, cleanse my heart, and prepare a place in the house with many mansions—the house of the Father. Thank You, Lord, that on the cross You accomplished everything to carry our—and also my—punishment; and that You have made me—yes, even me—a child of God. Hallelujah, what a Savior. Amen.'"

Afterword

The Corrie ten Boom House

Fulfilling Corrie ten Boom's dream of an "open house" like her family created, the Corrie ten Boom House and Museum in Haarlem, The Netherlands, was officially opened on April 15, 1988, exactly five years after Corrie's death. The house is less than an hour's trip by car or train from Amsterdam.

Amidst the bustling business district of Haarlem is the house that features the famous "hiding place," the basis of Corrie's well-known book and movie by the same name. The rooms are furnished as they were in the past, and there is also an exhibition about the Dutch resistance during World War II, along with a special display on Corrie's connection with the ministry of Trans World Radio. Just as when the Ten Boom family lived there, a clock and watch shop occupies the first floor—although it has since been modernized.

The house is operated by a foundation whose purpose is to keep the spiritual inheritance of the Ten Boom family alive as a sign and inspiration to present and future generations.

Tours through the house, located at 19 Barteljorisstraat, are given by volunteers (in English); operating hours are from 10 A.M. to 4 P.M. April 1–October 31, and from 11 A.M. to 3 P.M.

November 1–March 31. The house is closed on Sunday and Monday. Special appointments can be arranged for groups.

Admission to the house is free, although donations toward the continued preservation of the house are welcomed. All books written by or about Corrie ten Boom are available in the museum in various languages.

Corrie ten Boom House Haarlem Foundation
P.O. Box 2237
2002 CE Haarlem
The Netherlands
Tel: 31–23–5310823

Steps to Peace with God

Step 1 God's Purpose: Peace and Life

God loves you and wants you to experience peace and life—abundant and eternal.

The Bible Says . . .

"... we have peace with God through our Lord Jesus Christ." **Romans 5:1**

"For God so loved the world that He gave His only begotten Son, that whoever believes in Him should not perish but have everlasting life." **John 3:16**

"... I have come that they may have life, and that they may have it more abundantly." **John 10:10b**

Since God planned for us to have peace and the abundant life right now, why are most people not having this experience?

Step 2 Our Problem: Separation

God created us in His own image to have an abundant life. He did not make us as robots to automatically love and obey Him, but gave us a will and a freedom of choice.

We chose to disobey God and go our own willful way. We still make this choice today. This results in separation from God.

Our choice results in separation from God.

The Bible Says . . .

"For all have sinned and fall short of the glory of God." **Romans 3:23**

"For the wages of sin is death, but the gift of God is eternal life in Christ Jesus our Lord." **Romans 6:23**

People (Sinful)   God (Holy)

Our Attempts

There is only one remedy for this problem of separation.

Through the ages, individuals have tried in many ways to bridge this gap . . . without success . . .

The Bible Says . . .

"There is a way that seems right to man, but in the end it leads to death." Proverbs 14:12

"But your iniquities have separated you from God; and your sins have hidden His face from you, so that He will not hear." Isaiah 59:2

Step 3 God's Remedy: The Cross

Jesus Christ is the only answer to this problem. He died on the Cross and rose from the grave, paying the penalty for our sin and bridging the gap between God and people.

The Bible Says . . .

". . . God is on one side and all the people on the other side, and Christ Jesus, Himself man, is between them to bring them together . . ." 1 Timothy 2:5

"For Christ also has suffered once for sins, the just for the unjust, that He might bring us to God . . ." 1 Peter 3:18a

"But God demonstrates His own love for us in this: While we were still sinners, Christ died for us." Romans 5:8

God has provided the only way . . . we must make the choice . . .

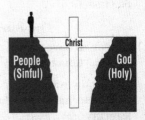

Step 4 | Our Response: Receive Christ

We must trust Jesus Christ and receive Him by personal invitation.

The Bible Says . . .

"Behold, I stand at the door and knock. If anyone hears My voice and opens the door, I will come in to him and dine with him, and he with Me." Revelation 3:20

"But as many as received Him, to them He gave the right to become children of God, even to those who believe in His name." John 1:12

". . . if you confess with your mouth the Lord Jesus and believe in your heart that God has raised Him from the dead, you will be saved." Romans 10:9

Are you here ... or here?

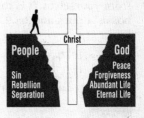

Is there any good reason why you cannot receive Jesus Christ right now?

How to receive Christ:

1. Admit your need (I am a sinner).
2. Be willing to turn from your sins (repent).
3. Believe that Jesus Christ died for you on the Cross and rose from the grave.
4. Through prayer, invite Jesus Christ to come in and control your life through the Holy Spirit. (Receive Him as Lord and Savior.)

What to Pray:

Dear Lord Jesus,

I know that I am a sinner and need Your forgiveness. I believe that You died for my sins. I want to turn from my sins. I now invite You to come into my heart and life. I want to trust and follow You as Lord and Savior.

In Jesus' name. Amen.

_____   _____
Date   Signature

God's Assurance:
His Word

If you prayed this prayer,

The Bible Says...

**"For 'whoever calls upon the name of the Lord will be saved.'"
Romans 10:13**

Did you sincerely ask Jesus Christ to come into your life? Where is He right now? What has He given you?

"For it is by grace you have been saved, through faith—and this is not from yourselves, it is the gift of God—not by works, so that no one can boast." Ephesians 2:8,9

The
Bible Says...

**"He who has the Son has life; he who does not have the Son of God does not have life. These things I have written to you who believe in the name of the Son of God, that you may know that you have eternal life, and that you may continue to believe in the name of the Son of God."
1 John 5:12–13, NKJV**

Receiving Christ, we are born into God's family through the supernatural work of the Holy Spirit who indwells every believer…this is called regeneration or the "new birth."

This is just the beginning of a wonderful new life in Christ. To deepen this relationship you should:

1. Read your Bible every day to know Christ better.
2. Talk to God in prayer every day.
3. Tell others about Christ.
4. Worship, fellowship, and serve with other Christians in a church where Christ is preached.
5. As Christ's representative in a needy world, demonstrate your new life by your love and concern for others.

God bless you as you do.

Billy Graham

If you want further help in the decision you have made, write to:
Billy Graham Evangelistic Association P.O. Box 779, Minneapolis, Minnesota 55440-0779